Awareness That Heals

Awareness That Heals

*Bringing Heart and Wisdom
to Life's Challenges*

ROBERT STROCK

www.TheGlobalBridge.org

THE GLOBAL BRIDGE FOUNDATION™

2021 Ocean Avenue Suite 202

Santa Monica, CA 90405

info@TheGlobalBridge.org

10 9 8 7 6 5 4 3 2

First Edition 2019

Printed in Canada

ISBN: 978-0-578-40215-4

Library of Congress Control Number: 2019902989

Table of Contents

A Note to the Reader

This book took quite a while to write. And during those years, I went back and forth, trying to decide whether it would be for therapists and educators, or for anyone who was sincerely looking to live a life that integrates life's challenges while activating a healing response simultaneously. Then, wanting to have the greatest impact, I ultimately decided to write to lay people and all seekers of greater peace—and not to the therapeutic community directly.

When the book was finished, it became clear that the exact same principles applied to both those who are in the field of psychology and those who aren't. In fact, those in the field could be the main proponents of passing on this approach to their students and clients.

Because the therapeutic community has such a profound impact on people's suffering, I have written the preface that follows, encouraging all of us as therapists and educators to bring these principles to our clients and students, *and* also to do this inner work ourselves. The lessons are the same, no matter what roles we play in life.

While the preface is specifically focused, the content of this book is all-inclusive, written as it is for lay people, therapists—and all of us. For we are, indeed, in the same boat.

Preface

A New Paradigm for Practicing Psychotherapy

As you preview the eight practices or tools, you will notice that every one of them can be relevant to you as a therapist or educator—and to you as a person.

Like you, I am deeply involved in the field of psychology and care deeply about its future. Whether you are a practicing psychotherapist who cares deeply about your clients, or an educator shaping the next generation of practitioners, I am sure you want to offer the most healing support possible for those clients and students. At the same time, we surely want to take care of our own well-being and that of those closest to us. This may sound straightforward and even obvious. But the book I am sharing with you suggests that, in fact, it is far more complicated and subtle than we think.

This is why I am reaching out to you personally with this book. I believe that the practices presented are not only good for our clients, but also good for us. They are as much about *living conscious, sensitive lives* as they are about *providing good therapy*. They are guides for how to live—for clients, for therapists, and for all of us.

The basis of the new paradigm is developing our capacity to find *awareness that heals.* Let me differentiate this clearly from what is generally understood as "awareness" in our field. The common definition of awareness is being in touch with, and seeing, what is happening to us emotionally. What this book explores is *awareness that sees both our emotional challenges and triggers our caring heart to support healing* at the same time. For example, if you visualize times when you've been angry or frightened, can you see how important (and difficult) it would be to turn in a healing direction when you are triggered or frozen?

In my training as a psychotherapist, I was always surprised at how little instruction was given on how we can respond at our times of greatest need. From my experience, most approaches to psychology—and programs that teach it—miss the fundamental element of this new paradigm. As you preview the eight practices or tools, you will notice that every one of them can be relevant to you as a therapist or educator—*and to you as a person.*

Since this broader view of awareness and the practices that guide us toward well-being are being defined as the very ground of mental health, our role as psychotherapists is to fertilize that ground by practicing in our personal lives the healing guidance that we're suggesting to our clients. I believe that each of the eight skills explored in these pages can help us understand how we can face what is most challenging and respond in ways that best take care of ourselves and others. But if you do not immediately accept this bold assertion, I completely understand. It was not until I was profoundly challenged by life that I realized how much I did not know.

I experienced this dilemma only after a quarter of a century as a psychotherapist—and only when my own life was turned upside down by a medical crisis. I believe the world around us is currently in a crisis as well. Just as I needed new practices to deal with my own personal challenges, so does the world. My goal in sharing this book with you is to have optimal positive impact on our profession, our country and our world. It is my heartfelt wish to support this priority in our profession.

Acknowledgments

It will be hard to convey the degree to which I am grateful to so many people. The extra gratitude has to do with what a poor writer I am by myself, and how much skillful help was needed to make the practices easily accessible in writing. I say this with friendliness and honesty. There are five people who have written "me" better than I can write myself. They didn't change the ideas, nor did they allow their egos to get in the way—they simply made me clearer and more sequential. If you like the book, you'll be grateful you didn't have to read just what I wrote.

Dave Knapp, my dearest friend for over forty-five years, has been a rewriter of every chapter and every effort for the thirty-five years it has taken to move this book to greater clarity and simplification. We are so close it seems almost silly to thank him because we have been so connected in almost all aspects of life.

The other four are Lois Rose, Sasha Allenby, Judy Schwartz, and Mark Gerzon. They have each gone through the whole book more than once, and in some cases more than twenty times. It has truly been a community effort—unique in my life. I love each of them dearly for their contributions and far beyond.

More dear friends have edited and gone through many of the chapters and elements that they particularly specialize in. They are Shelley Pearce, Marilyn Levine, Patricia Bisch, Dr. Ken Druck, and Dr. Ken Blanchard. They all hung in there with me, especially at critical junctures of the book's development.

There are several other close friends and family members that have made significant and specific contributions. I give great thanks and appreciation to Michael Solomon, Keegan Bisch, Brent Kessel, and Justin Strock.

I also thank Michael Green for patiently developing the cover, Matthew Greenblatt for advising me on everything from the writing to all the next steps needed, and Mark Spiro for the music that helped carry me through the whole book and guided meditations.

Introduction

Shortly before my fiftieth birthday, my world was turned upside down, and my identity inside out. An inherited condition had reached a critical point and I had a kidney transplant. For most people, this is normally the great news, but I had major complications from the medications necessary to keep my one kidney alive.

For the first time in a life I'd experienced as fulfilling and fortunate, I became profoundly disoriented. I couldn't access my heart and my normal vital energy. I couldn't even feel the gratitude toward my brother who gave me the kidney, even though I knew it was very much there. Instead of my mostly stable experience of love and gratitude for being alive, I was agitated, exhausted and empty. I was afraid these losses were permanent, and to some extent they were: there was no way to anticipate what was to become of me.

Up to that point, I had faced and dealt with reasonably well the normal challenges of modern life; I had also been blessed with considerable fulfillment and success. In addition to a wonderful family and good health, I had a flourishing psychotherapy practice in Los Angeles. Over the years I had developed physical, psychological and contemplative methods for fostering balance and inner peace. Not only my own life, but also the lives of hundreds of clients with whom I had worked, seemed to be proof that I had learned what I needed to know. I had been fulfilled with bringing qualities such as love, peace, trust, strength and compassion into my own life and to the lives of those around me. I had believed that—with good intentions, therapeutic support and spiritual practice—these qualities were almost guaranteed.

But then, that world vanished. I felt profound grief about losing the life that I had had. My core emotional identity seemed to have dissolved. It was as though I'd had a "heartectomy": I felt as if my heart had been taken away.

"Who is this person?" I would ask myself. "What has happened to me?"

Because of the medications I was taking to prevent my kidney from being rejected, the resulting severe insomnia and exhaustion, and the need for further medications to deal with these side effects, I had little or no control over how I felt. I meditated and prayed, and I used my therapeutic strategies—but I just felt worse than ever.

No matter how hard I tried to feel good, I was helpless and unable to get there. The very medications that were enabling me to survive were now undermining my quality of life, and it wasn't good news. The new bottom line was: life was *not* great and good. In fact, at times, life was hell.

What on earth could I do? I was afraid that I would never be able to feel at peace or fulfilled in my heart again.

In this book, I share with you eight practices, most of which were either created or deepened as a result of this crisis. I had the added motivation to develop these practices because *my well-being, perhaps even my life, depended on them.*

I have found that even if we are content in life, there are inevitably at least one or two areas where we have a need to develop ourselves in order to deepen our sense of well-being. And as we do this, we have to *learn* how to open to our human side—open to what hurts, frightens or angers us. Allowing ourselves to experience our need for support in these moments maximizes our chances for greater peace.

I stress the word *learn*, because, as my chemical crisis revealed, I wasn't prepared for a challenge at this level. Sharing with others had always been my natural inclination, and that was how I'd always resolved anything that was really disturbing to me. My life had been full of deep and meaningful communication with friends and those I loved, and this had always provided greater acceptance, peace and intimacy. Now, however, the sharing didn't have the healing effect it had always had. I couldn't feel the heart qualities that I was routinely used to accessing. The loss of this deep source of well-being was devastating. I was facing a completely different kind of challenge where I was chemically imbalanced. No matter how well I communicated or was cared for by others, I was not able to feel anywhere near the sense of well-being that I was used to.

After months of anguish, I started to discover new ways to support myself, which eventually evolved into ways to be more at peace with whatever state I was in. It became clear to me then that what I'd learned could be useful to everyone I cared about and, of course, my clients—and hopefully you too. I know, from their experience and my own, that we can live in a more supportive way—no matter how difficult our feelings are—if we cultivate these practices. The first is what I call *awareness that heals*, which is foundational for all the others.

THE PRACTICES ARE:
- **Accessing Awareness That Heals**
- **Cultivating Friendly Mind**
- **Moving from Self-Rejection toward Self-Compassion**
- **Inquiring from the Heart**
- **Developing Wisdom Guidance**
- **Tuning into Tone of Voice**
- **Moving from Feelings to Needs**
- **Transforming Anger into Intimacy and Strength**

These practices will support you to develop self-caring and the capacity to respond in an effective way to life's challenges, especially at times when you are most prone to be critical or to withdraw. This can happen with your willingness to (1) discover and examine your challenging emotions and life situations, (2) begin to access a place inside that *wants* to care for you when you feel the most hopeless, and (3) to develop any of the practices that will best guide you to healing qualities and actions. If you commit to these steps, which are so often avoided or unseen, I promise you, based not only on my own experience, but also that of scores of friends and clients, that your life will be more fulfilling in several specific ways. Here are some of the key benefits of these practices:

- You will learn how to combine awareness of your challenges with a core need to move toward healing so that this awareness that heals becomes a grounded pathway leading toward your sense of well-being.

- When you reject yourself, subtly or not, this book will provide tools to discover where you usually and unwittingly abandon or criticize yourself. You will also learn strategies that will help you develop self-caring instead of self-rejection.

- You will learn how to be proficient in asking yourself beneficial questions when you are in great pain and fear; they will help you navigate through these toughest times in your life.

- You will discover the ways to access and utilize your own wisest inner guidance—especially in times of greatest need.

- You will become more aware of your tone of voice and how it can create harm; you will also learn how it can be used as an instrument to bring you much closer to your heart and to express to others the healing that can be conveyed in the tones you discover.

- You will learn to identify your feelings and your needs and to distinguish between them. You will also learn to make a direct link between your most difficult feelings and your corresponding core needs. Being able to do this will catalyze the greatest healing.

- You will discover new ways of escaping the trap of repetitive and destructive patterns where you've acted out your anger and aggressive emotion. You'll learn how to pivot from being *against* someone or something, to discovering and being supportive of your underlying needs.

- You will learn a whole new way of using your friendly thoughts to guide you when you see no answers or solutions and feel overcome by your emotions. You will see how your friendly mind can support you no matter what you are facing or feeling.

Some Helpful Hints as You Read

When I use *we* and talk about *our* lives and experiences, I am writing about an area where I'm still very much working on myself and growing. When I speak to *you* or talk about *your* life, it is because we're dealing with areas or practices that I've mostly integrated into my life, and I feel I have a familiarity with practicing them by now.

The we-you distinction is particularly important because there are so many approaches, techniques and teachings that don't reveal the personal work on the part of the creator. I believe this lack of exposed vulnerability unwittingly reinforces a desire for us to seek the impossible—a complete resolution or answer for ourselves—in some of life's greatest challenges. It is a core principle in this book to both guide and model how we can all, including myself, care for the kind of challenges that we have without having to *get over them*. Here, I'm referring to those elements of life that we can't control, such as the behavior of others, profound loss, or capacities that are limited due to aging.

I hope that both the "*we*" and the "*you*" discussions and all they entail will support you to accept, and be kinder toward, what you can't change.

- I ask you to read this book not just as a reader, but also as a participator: let yourself get personally involved. Just as I have brought my life's challenges to these practices, I am inviting you to bring yours. You will derive the greatest benefit if you identify at least one personal challenge, whether past, present or anticipated, and bring it to your experience as you read *Awareness That Heals*. If you follow this suggestion, each practice will make more sense and the experience of reading will be more real and relevant. Your personal involvement enhances the dynamic relationship between the practices and you.

- To support you, there are **Reflection Points** throughout the book that invite you to apply these practices directly to your life. Similarly, at the end of each chapter, I offer you questions to ask yourself so that the practice itself can become more meaningful and benefit your life in practical ways.

- At the back of the book, you will find a section entitled **Introspective Guides**. These guides, in the form of charts, support seeing our feelings and core needs more clearly. They are free and available to download or order in laminated form at the book's website: www. AwarenessThatHeals.org. They give key assistance as you read the book and can be used in whatever way you find most beneficial afterwards.

- On the website I have provided **Guided Meditations** for each of the practices. They will give you a clear summary of the content, and allow for your personal experience to be felt more deeply in your body and heart. They are especially helpful if you listen *both before and after* you read. All of the meditations will remain available for you to consult long after you have read the book.

- This book invites you to read it as both client and therapist, both student and teacher. You will feel supported to find the courage and humility to be emotionally honest with yourself and also be accepting and caring toward what is difficult. At times, as the student, you might feel inadequate or frightened, but the teacher in you will be supported to be contemplative and to find your wisest voice to bring you toward healing and well-being. As a client, you might feel overwhelmed or disoriented, but as a counselor, you can comfort and guide yourself with greater compassion.

So now let's turn to the first practice, which is *Accessing Awareness That Heals.*

Accessing Awareness That Heals

*You can use your awareness—this awareness that heals—
in a new and compelling way that will support you to see
clearly what is challenging you and to find the intention
to care for yourself at the same time.*

My life and my work have taught me one fundamental lesson: there is a place inside each of us that knows, cares, and is able to guide us on the healing journey of our unique life. When it comes to our unfolding as a person, this place, which I call *awareness that heals*, is our most powerful asset. This chapter will help us access this awareness and return to it whenever we face challenges in our life.

What is the place, this invaluable resource that rests within each of us? What exactly do I mean by awareness that heals?

It means being able to *notice accurately what is happening when we are challenged, and then to respond with a sincere intention to support healing and well-being.*

Awareness, in my definition, does not mean a cold, clinical, "neutral" staring-in-the-mirror type of self-knowledge. That kind of detached, uninvolved self-observation almost never supports what we truly need.

The path to the awareness I am inviting you to take is different. I am proposing that you include, and even embrace, the challenges, the pain, the regrets, rejection and resistances that you may have experienced or are experiencing. *By accepting what you are feeling, rather than rejecting or ignoring those feelings, they actually become guideposts on your journey toward what you need.*

I am introducing this concept of awareness that heals because awareness by itself is not enough. We can frequently be aware of something, sometimes for years or even decades, but that awareness doesn't reliably change anything. If we look at moments in our lives when we identified that we were angry, hurt or frightened, most of the time this awareness did not catalyze within us a movement for healing or change. This becomes more evident when we see that we are still stuck in the trap of being aware of our anger and remaining in the same emotional place. You can use your awareness—this awareness that heals—in a new and compelling way that will support you to experience greater peace and fulfillment in your life.

As we begin to explore this, I invite you to identify at least one area of your life that is challenging to you—one that is most central to your life in the present—and keep it in mind as we work together. (Perhaps it is the one that you chose as you read the introduction.) This will make what we do more meaningful for you.

One of the first differentiations that came clear to me as I worked with this concept is that "awareness" and "unawareness" are not two opposing states. On the contrary, they are on a continuum. I have simplified that continuum by identifying four levels of awareness.

LEVEL 1:	**Awareness of Being Unaware**
LEVEL 2:	**Fleeting Awareness**
LEVEL 3:	**Intellectual Awareness**
LEVEL 4:	**Awareness That Heals**

The first three levels are necessary and catalytic building blocks that move us toward the gold: transformational healing. It is on the fourth level that we access the awareness that truly heals, and where our great human potential can be realized.

LEVEL 1

Awareness of Being Unaware

The first level of awareness is becoming aware of, and respecting, that we have an unconscious that limits the quality of our lives. It is realizing we have a vast world inside and outside ourselves that we have yet to discover. This insight offers us inspiration, urging us toward that desire to wake up.

In this level, we become aware that we have been unaware of many things. It's a crucial starting point because when we operate from the assumption that we know what's going on inside ourselves, we don't have the curiosity or the alertness that is most often necessary to initiate the vital motivation to grow and to heal.

Becoming aware of our unawareness is often viewed as something negative. We frequently, and often unconsciously, have the belief that if we feel and look like we are aware, we will appear more "together" in the eyes of the outside world and be more at peace with ourselves. We tend to see ourselves as a failure when we have not been aware of something. However, this moving from being unaware of our unawareness to developing this more humble awareness allows us to see major parts of ourselves that are hidden from us. This is a breakthrough every time it occurs.

Starting out on this journey of awareness, we may not even know we are unaware. When we take a closer look at ourselves, we begin to face the parts of ourselves that have been unseen, ignored or avoided. Here are some samples:

- We realize that our tone of voice, almost without our knowing it, is expressing anger, or irritation.
- We suddenly recognize that we have been behaving in a confrontational or argumentative way and we hadn't seen it before.
- We have been feeling helpless in a relationship, but it has become so normalized that we haven't put our attention on it for a long while.
- We feel withdrawn or empty, but it has become so habitual that we barely recognize how painful it is.
- We think we are sad, but actually we are angry.
- We think we are expressing one emotion but have been totally unaware that another emotion is being expressed.
- We feel alone and don't know how to be more connected, both inside and outside of ourselves.

As these examples illustrate, the starting point for Level One is *becoming aware that we have been unaware*. We start to recognize that we, and virtually everyone around us, have areas of unawareness that negatively affect the quality of our lives. This in itself is an evolutionary, motivating—and empowering—insight. For many of us, it represents a monumental shift. If we can embrace and appreciate this essential basic step, we will be moving toward living a more purposeful and growth-inspired life.

At this point, the focus on awareness creates a new depth of curiosity. You may find yourself asking something like, "What areas of unawareness are causing the most suffering in my life and how can I pay more attention to what is needed?"

▼

Reflection Point: Do you remember a time when you misinterpreted either your own or your partner's feelings, and it resulted in conflict? (This question can be applied to your current relationship or to a previous one.)

Taking It Deeper: Do you remember a time when you said something important to another and were surprised at the negative response you received? And when you put it in the context, can you take a step back and see if you were coming across during this time in a way that could have contributed to this reaction?

LEVEL 2
Fleeting Awareness

The second level is experienced as glimpses of awareness that are brief epiphanies of insight—the moments we see, or sense, elements that are missing from our lives or keeping us from changes we want to make. Usually these insights are so startling or difficult that we quickly lose our focus. This is because we are afraid that focusing on them, and then acting on them, will create more conflict, disruption or risk than we can handle. As a result we swiftly, and mostly unconsciously, suppress them.

This fleeting awareness may occur occasionally or repeatedly in your everyday experience. You may notice, when your intimate partner sees and asks about something going on with you, that you deny the insecurity that you're experiencing. You may see it for a brief instant, but then quickly turn your focus on their insensitivity. Another time you might notice your breathing is very shallow or that you are holding your breath, and when you focus on this, you have a momentary awareness of feeling diminished by someone important to you or by something that happened—but the insight is too painful to sustain. Alternatively, you may have received repeated feedback from those around you about something you haven't seen in yourself, and you get a quick flash of your own anger, irritability or defensiveness. However, you aren't able to stay focused on this reaction long enough to do something about it.

See if you recognize yourself in any of the following examples of fleeting awareness:

- You realize that when you get angry, withdrawn or impatient, you almost immediately lose sight of it.
- When you feel competitive with your partner, you see it in a flash. But the awareness is lost as you return to your usual mode of being in denial or fighting about an unrelated issue.
- You glimpse that you are anxious deep down inside. But then you distract yourself by getting dissatisfied with yourself, your partner or other parts of your life.
- You experience a feeling of anxiety or inadequacy that you go in and out of noticing.
- You notice a deep love or gratitude for the most important people in your life. But before you can express it, something intervenes and you never say it.
- You find yourself thinking about your own mortality, but quickly become uncomfortable and push it away.

What if, in each of the examples above, we could have sustained our fleeting awareness long enough to bring it into the open? Perhaps then we could have allowed ourselves to be in touch with this intuition and aspects of our lives we are yearning for. What if we could accept that a new awareness is often a call to connect with our lives in a deeper, more fulfilling way? If we can sustain our fleeting awareness and begin to integrate it into our lives, then we are ready to experience the next level of awareness.

LEVEL 3
Intellectual Awareness

At the third level, our awareness begins to stabilize intellectually. We recognize what we feel, but we are not yet able to guide ourselves in a healing direction.

Intellectual awareness is useful as we wake up to patterns that consistently have caused us suffering. It is a necessary catalytic building block taking us another step closer to including the key beneficial element, which, in almost all situations, is the intention to move toward healing and well-being. In other words, you have a stable awareness about something instead of the fleeting awareness that you had in the second level. However, similar to a fleeting awareness, it still doesn't motivate you to do much about it. You might hear yourself saying, "I'm aware of my anger toward my partner," or "I'm afraid of talking about my sexual insecurities or needs." You notice what is occurring but your awareness at this stage doesn't motivate you to respond in a healing way.

Having an intellectual awareness is often considered to be very useful on its own. It is very common for those of us who are on a therapeutic or spiritual path to give too much weight to this third level of awareness. As we do this and we access our intellectual awareness of thoughts, feelings and patterns, we often feel a confidence in its ability to transform our challenges that is, in the end, misplaced. We might say to ourselves, "Wow, now that I am aware of this negative pattern, I'm sure things will get better!" It is a kind of wishful thinking: it's as if we believe that the awareness *itself* will solve the challenges we are facing.

Of course, it is inherently helpful to see our patterns. But unfortunately, at Level Three, this awareness has yet to become truly meaningful because it is not connected to a sincere and stable motivation to heal.

Here are some ways either my clients or I have experienced this level of awareness:

- I was aware I was frustrated. In spite of my efforts to the contrary, I stayed frustrated and carried on being irritable toward my partner. I just couldn't move out of that state of agitation.
- I noticed that I needed to be kinder, but I didn't have the courage or depth of humility to admit it.
- I was hurt that my partner was not giving me the appreciation, understanding or companionship I wanted, but I was too afraid that if I asked for it directly it would lead to conflict or rejection.
- I wanted to admit to a friend that I was feeling anxious, but I was too embarrassed to expose my vulnerability.
- I'm very aware that I want to bring inspiration to my life by doing something for the world, but other desires continuously distract me.

When we only have an intellectual awareness of these challenging feelings, it can feel like we are living wounded on an island that appears to have no resources for healing. We might use words like *hypnotized* or *frozen* to describe these moments. Most of us don't actually realize that the only hope for not being isolated on this island is to learn how to be present with our own painful feelings as we seek healing options.

Existing exclusively at the third level of awareness almost inevitably leaves us feeling like we are caught in a dead end of painful feelings—and we can't see a way out. Because this level doesn't actually lead to any significant healing, it is no wonder that we might have a tendency to turn away from these feelings or suppress them. If we aren't given, or can't find, real guidance on how we can take better care of ourselves at these times, there is limited relief in just noticing our distressing emotions.

Reflection Point: Can you identify an area where: you are intellectually aware of a feeling; you don't like the way you continue to express or experience it; but you still see yourself repeating it—and you can't see any viable options for taking better care of yourself?

Taking It Deeper: In your love relationships, what is your most frequent pattern that you see intellectually, but haven't been able to find a way to make changes toward healing and fulfillment?

LEVEL 4
Awareness That Heals

At this fourth level, we are not only aware of our present challenging feelings, but we experience a genuine motivation to move toward healing. The moment that these two states—awareness of our challenges and our intention to heal—are simultaneously recognized, we have the best of both worlds. We experience awareness that heals: we honor a difficult human experience by being aware without judgment, and at the same time, we focus on supporting and guiding ourselves toward well-being and ways to access what will benefit us.

These are moments of great purpose as being aware of the source of suffering can be used to support our healing. This is life changing—we are now at a pivotal turning point. These times are often experienced with great aliveness as we are moved by this epiphany or *Aha!* moment that is both grounded in the acceptance of what is difficult and inspired by our compassionate responses. We find ourselves contemplating how we can respond with healing actions and attitudes.

Here are a few examples that bring awareness that heals to life:

- You become aware that you are afraid to approach someone you're attracted to. Despite awareness of your fear, you're able to focus on finding your courage to pursue this potential love relationship.
- You notice that you feel confused about why you keep picking incompatible partners. You can feel your need to do otherwise and this leads you to contemplating the qualities that a potential partner would need to have for you to have the best chance for finding a more fulfilling relationship.
- You listen to your tone of voice and you hear that it is totally lacking in heart connection, making you sound like an overconfident expert. This leads you to looking within at how you can speak with more sensitivity.
- You are wounded by a friend's sarcasm that is directed at you. You know you don't want to just react and you look for a heartfelt response that is going to support your friendship.

As you can see from each of the above examples, the fourth level of awareness, unlike the first three, is a powerful path for taking the next step toward healing. For the first time, our awareness is coupled with our intention to heal and supporting us to take the next practical steps. We are aware of what challenges us and are wholeheartedly dedicated to doing our best to meet those challenges.

In our physical world, when we are hungry, this level of awareness will automatically lead us to do what comes naturally, and we will eat. If we are tired, we sleep. If we require medical help, we will seek it.

This applies to our inner world as well. If we are sad, we can see and take actions or change attitudes that lead us toward happiness. If we are angry, we can see we are lacking in equilibrium or strength, and we take the necessary steps that will lead us toward what is needed. Awareness that heals enables us to identify aspects of incompleteness inside ourselves and use this awareness as a motivation to lead us in the direction of fulfillment. We can't heal our suffering if we aren't deeply aware of it. When we access awareness that heals, our personal challenges are brought, in a very real and practical way, to our intention to heal.

Living from this fourth level of awareness is similar to the response you have to hearing a baby cry. When she does, you would naturally check to see if she was hungry, needed a diaper changed, was sick, or in need of loving care. We can learn to give our own emotions this kind of response—we can see them like infants that need the same loving and tender attention.

Why do we reach to help a baby, but don't have the same reaction toward ourselves? The answer is that we don't recognize that experiencing vulnerable emotions is the same message calling us to awaken to what we need. Consciously or unconsciously, we may believe that we should have outgrown these reactions by now. The problem is that we haven't, and we are being insensitive to ourselves to believe that we don't need support at these times. Recognizing and developing this caring attitude toward all of our challenging feelings can foster the desire to support a healing intention in our times of need. This capacity for self-care exists only in ourselves. No one else can ever do it for us.

When we access awareness that heals, we do the best work on ourselves. Every time we are aware of our deepest challenges and are in touch with a yearning to unite with our heart's purest qualities and actions, we connect with that central place of purpose within us. This can help us to transform our lives and relationships. When we have a conflict, we can lead with an intention to heal as soon as possible, which means we will be moving toward whatever beneficial qualities and actions are most needed at that moment. It's then that possibilities for experiencing deeper, balanced and more loving relationships reveal themselves.

To give you a glimpse of the potential that awareness that heals has to connect you to your essential needs as you address life's challenges, here is a personal case study provided by my colleague, Carol.

Carol

I was sitting watching TV when I had the urge for ice cream. I began to eat it and didn't stop until I had eaten almost the whole pint.

At this point, the second level of awareness was activated. I had a fleeting awareness that I felt like a failure, but I didn't know why I felt that way at the time. I realized I was about to let it pass as usual but instead of doing so, I stopped. "Wait! Let's look at what's happening here. I'm in my pattern. I frequently reach for food when I feel inadequate. What if I take a look at what's there more closely?"

From my past history, feelings of failure most frequently show up around men. This is an extension of having a very difficult relationship with my father growing up. At this point I couldn't figure out what the specifics were that triggered me. So I thought back a couple of days and remembered that I had received a message from a recent boyfriend who sensitively addressed an unresolved issue. This is where I started to activate the third level of awareness.

He had written a deep and heartfelt email to me and I had only responded to it with two brief sentences. I began to realize that underlying this feeling was a sense that I was defective and unlovable. I had the intention to send warmth to myself and to him, which was the beginning of the fourth level of awareness.

Next I remembered that I had been working on being able to more fully experience the qualities of trust and faith in myself that were deeply wounded. I saw that as a child I was stopped from both speaking my true feelings with my father and most importantly from trusting myself. Once I saw this link, I wrote a much deeper and more heartfelt email to my ex than the two-sentence one that I had sent to him. I allowed myself to express my depth of caring for him, as well as the areas where I felt like I had fallen short in the past. I met him at the same heart level that he had shown to me. The peace and love inside me were so strong, and so profound, that I no longer had the feeling that had driven me to polish off almost a whole pint of ice cream.

What Carol did wasn't easy. It required her to be aware of her past wounds while feeling them in the present. Because she could access awareness that heals, she could find strategies to respond to these challenges. Meeting the deepest challenges of our lives with a wish to move toward healing and compassion will always require some contemplation and some heartfelt encouragement.

Where Awareness That Heals Guides Us

Once we've accessed our awareness that heals, we naturally look for what will be healing or create a sense of well-being. Sometimes it is possible that, just by being in touch with the awareness of our challenges and contemplating a way to support ourselves and others, we can discover, activate and focus on the particular healing quality or actions we need. But the majority of the time we will need a practice to help us *identify our essential needs and to experience the essential qualities that are most healing in our unique situation.*

I call these needs and qualities (such as acceptance, kindness, courage, trust, and many more) "essential" because they inherently fulfill attributes of our heart and the finest parts of our character. Accessing them will be a central focus throughout the book. They are internal states that reveal themselves as the most fulfilling and compassionate part of our nature. They are key to our mental health and spiritual well-being. In this book, I gave needs and qualities exactly the same meaning because I want to relate to you, whatever your orientation is. If, for example, your background is more psychological, it would likely be much more natural for you to think in terms of "needs," as in a need for empathy or a need for love. If your background is more spiritual, you might be more familiar with the word "quality," and you would most likely identify empathy or love as qualities.

The practices in the next seven chapters were created to reach these core-enriching parts of our nature. When we are in touch with them or even focusing on them within ourselves, we experience what can be described as being on our way home.

For example, we may be aware of feeling afraid or frustrated but be unable to identify or access the essential quality or need that will support healing. There is a comprehensive chart (also available for download at www.AwarenessThatHeals.org) in the **Introspective Guides** section at the back of the book entitled **From Challenging Feelings to Essential Qualities and Needs**. Its purpose is to make it easier for you to identify what you need when you are facing any difficult challenges. I've taken some of the more common emotions and qualities/needs from the chart and created the sample list below: it will give you a beginning sense of these connections. As you peruse them, you will see that we usually need more than one essential quality to support our healing. The process can be gradual or immediate, depending on your situation. We will be exploring this in later practices.

Challenging Emotion	Corresponding Essential Qualities or Needs
Distrust	Contemplation/Trust
Fear	Courage/Safety
Frustration	Tolerance/Acceptance
Grief	Tolerance/Empathy
Guilt	Accountability/Innocence
Helplessness	Acceptance/Discipline
Hurt	Tolerance/Kindness
Impatience	Tolerance/Harmlessness
Inadequacy	Tolerance/Growth
Regret	Acceptance/Growth
Tension	Tolerance/Relaxation

Using awareness that heals to connect to your essential qualities may or may not be a new concept for you; however, whether it is or not, I think you would agree that it is an easy one to intellectually understand and a hard one to continually practice! As you strengthen your commitment to practicing, it is essential not to let ordinary feelings of discouragement or failure stop the flow of your motivation and inspiration. The chapter that follows will show you the practice that will allow you to do just that.

The more you can recognize and access your awareness that heals, the more instinctual it will become. With much practice, it can shift from being a fully conscious intentional process to something you do as if it's second nature. If you devote yourself to finding a healing intention, you can find yourself automatically engaging awareness and your wish to be compassionate shortly after being triggered. You can eventually move into it without even consciously realizing you have done so.

In other words, your emotional reactions are no longer the primary place that you have to respond from. Instead, your awareness and your healing responses (thoughts, qualities and actions) take on more and more significance, becoming more central to your sense of self and identity than the initial feelings and the thoughts themselves.

Key Messages

We've seen that there are important areas of our lives that we are unaware of and the inestimable significance of how becoming aware creates a path for healing. It is only by being aware of what we've been unaware of that we can most profoundly grow and evolve. This understanding is the driving force and the motivation to notice and have curiosity about what we might have missed in the past.

We also have seen that, even when we do get glimpses of our challenges, we can suppress them—and when we do that, we suppress not only those glimpses, but also the healing that could happen. We usually do this because we fear, most of the time on an unconscious level, that we won't be able to face these challenges in a sustained way, or that the consequences of acting on what we see are too threatening.

We explored the significant limitations of the belief that intellectual awareness of our challenges will in itself bring us healing. There is no way to overstate the importance of this insight as it is the key turning point to move us from being stuck to what can bring healing.

If you take any single message from this book, it is to remember to focus on and access your innate intention to heal when challenged in any way. Developing awareness that heals will make all the difference in your life because it will help you to truly make the best out of whatever challenges life brings you. It also will encourage you to check in with yourself more often because, instead of being afraid of what will be revealed, you will discover a greater trust in your own way of supporting yourself. This will lead you to look for the most natural way to move toward the qualities of life that will be most healing and fulfilling.

Integrating the Chapter: Inquiries

On the following page—and in each chapter—are inquiries that will further support you to apply the practices to your life. Please don't use them to judge or measure yourself, but rather as a way to deeply reflect upon where you currently are, and to maximize your potential for beneficial outcomes from your intention to heal. I invite you to stay with the questions until you have been able to activate genuine curiosity.

Guidelines for Inquiry from the Heart

Exercise: Spend 3-5 minutes asking yourself each question either alone or with a partner. Just one recommendation: if you work with a partner, it is better for you both to fully read the guidelines.

Allow yourself to be silent for a period of time. Don't try and "answer" the question straight away. The inquiries are designed to trigger an ongoing process within you, rather than single answers. If you don't try to come up with a quick answer, and allow this silent contemplation, inquiry will give you a good chance to go deeply into yourself to access your intuition and will bring surprises that arise from your own realizations.

During and after working with a question, write down the most important insights and healing elements that you hear so that you will have a lasting and accessible understanding of where you are.

If you decide to do this work with a partner, make sure your partner remains neutral without facial expression and just listens, so that there are no distractions. Also, make it clear to your partner whether or not you want any feedback at the end. They need to do the same for you.

Integrating the Chapter: Inquiries

1. Have you seen any places where you have a fleeting awareness of a challenging emotion and where you are most likely to be able to support more healing to occur? Which one do you want to keep your focus on?

2. For what specific situation in your life do you most need to develop an intention to heal? Can you see what qualities and actions you need to focus on?

3. Select the emotions that have been difficult for you throughout your life, and choose one that has been the most challenging and is still active within you. How much has it been in your awareness through the years and what is the quality that you most need to help you with it?

4. Which qualities do you aspire to bring more into your life?

For additional support and further integration of Practice One, I strongly encourage you to listen to the guided meditations at www.AwarenessThatHeals.org.

Cultivating Friendly Mind

*When you can't find a way to Awareness
That Heals, how much is your mind a
friend—or an enemy?*

Very few of us are truly capable of staying supportive of ourselves at
these times. This is especially the case when faced with difficult life
conditions that we aren't prepared for or that are unexpected. Often, we
believe there is nothing we can do or that there is no way we can respond.
We feel stymied or paralyzed when we're most hurting, afraid or angry. At
these important and pivotal moments, we all could use the support of our
own friendly *realistic* thoughts instead of the ones that are self-critical and
make a bad situation worse.

How often have you found yourself feeling bad or thinking about
yourself in a critical way and thought, "I wish I knew what I could do
to best take care of myself"? Wouldn't it be priceless to have a way of
finding the right thoughts or actions that would be healing during times
of troublesome feelings? This guidance, and what is necessary to receive it,
is a major part of what we will explore together in this chapter.

But first, why wouldn't we want to support ourselves to find effective or skillful ways to respond to life's challenges? It's natural that we want to minimize our pain and suffering and maximize our healing and well-being. As normal as this may sound, very few of us have had anyone show us how to do it.

Prior to my kidney transplant and the ensuing inner chaos it created, my mind and my emotional state were in sync with each other. However, post-transplant, because of the impact of the unusual side effects of the medications, the contrast was dramatic—and often very disturbing. As I've described, my sense of well-being, which I could always count on before, was on "life-support" and I was in survival mode. It was during this time that I developed what I came to call *Friendly Mind: a way of thinking grounded, supportive thoughts, especially when life is most difficult and they are needed the most*. It felt natural to call it that because it is mobilized specifically at the times when we think we've done all we can do, and we still can't find a way to feel a sense of well-being.

Friendly mind is the *capacity to focus on our response to how we feel more than on the feeling itself*. It is a supportive inner space—a "friendly place" that guides us to the best way of taking care of ourselves no matter how challenging or even hopeless the situation may be.

Instead of being taken over by the negative impacts of emotions, medications, hormones, chemistry, or circumstances, friendly mind—as the term suggests—supports us with our own befriending thoughts. Even though we will not always be able to *feel* friendly because of the depth of the difficulties we are facing, it's possible to generate friendly guiding thoughts no matter what we feel.

This wasn't easy for me to get to at first. It came with fits and starts as I struggled to keep exhaustion, anxiety and irritability from taking over my life and mind. When I could generate and listen to my friendly thoughts and mind as I was feeling the worst, it turned out to make all the difference in the world.

During this most challenging time of my life, this shift was transformational: even though I couldn't *feel good*, I could find and experience a response to my plight that had a friendly understanding. Learning to "shift gears" into friendly mind not only affected the way that I handled my own situation, but it also changed the way I worked with clients.

But let me make clear to you, as I do with my clients, that friendly mind is not a quick-fix, three-easy-steps kind of technique. To make any change in life endure, practice and authenticity are required. But, as both my clients and I have come to know, it is worth the effort.

There is rarely an hour that goes by when our friendly mind is not beneficial either in addressing our more obvious habitual critical thoughts or dealing with life's greater challenges where the stakes are higher. At extremely challenging times it's so hard—perhaps even impossible—to feel at ease or even close to anything like peace. Having friendly guiding thoughts as our companions as we contemplate our next step is an enormous help. Friendly mind encourages us to move toward simple guiding thoughts and questions. These could be:

- "What's the best move for me in the next hour?"
- "I've heard that critical thought so many times and I'm asking for what would be helpful."
- "I am sorry you have to go through this—how can I best care for you now?"

Friendly mind doesn't exist to impose a new moral standard and create pressure of any kind. Instead, your friendly mind is *you* guiding yourself with thoughts that are empathic and understanding from the most sensible place inside. You are simply seeking what is, in your own eyes, a relaxed and natural next move—and if nothing is possible, then you seek to support acceptance and patience until you can find direction. This direction most frequently is to accept that you can't change the situation or feeling in that moment. You focus your thinking on how to respond to the situation in a helpful way, instead of trying to find solutions that, in that moment, are impossible.

Recognizing the Trap of Impossible Standards

Your friendly mind is there for you in a key way—it helps you recognize when you are trying to live up to an *impossible* or *unrealistic standard*— one that you have little or no hope of achieving at the present time or in the near future, or one that maybe you shouldn't be aspiring to live up to at all. When we have made our very best effort and have still not met that standard, it is unfortunately all too common for us to be critical toward ourselves. It is only when we look at it with our friendly mind that we realize that it doesn't make sense to give ourselves a hard time for not living up to those impossible or unrealistic standards.

A painful irony is that *when we pursue the impossible, we lose opportunities to do the possible.* There are many feelings and physiological states that make it very hard to feel good toward and about ourselves. Most of us can't easily feel joy when we're exhausted, or inspiration when we're down. This is so common and very much why having access to friendly thoughts is especially important in times of our greatest need.

It's important to know that even when you have understood that you deserve to have friendly thoughts, that doesn't mean that you will be able to implement them immediately. Old standards and habits have a way of sticking around, even when we know better. It takes time to welcome friendly mind.

Life's conditions are always changing, but all too often we don't adapt our expectations and desires to them. Our unawareness of what's needed at times of change is the source of so much extra pain. We impose prior standards on ourselves and fail to see the self-inflicted wounds that result from that. It is so important to lose the unrealistic promise of the standards we hold on to. We need to scrutinize them and ask, "In this particular circumstance in my life, do these standards really still apply?"

Reflection Point: Can you see an impossible or unrealistic standard operating in your life and identify specific critical thoughts you've said to yourself because of it?

Taking It Deeper: What could you say to yourself in response to these critical thoughts that might be helpful?

Most of these standards are internalized when we are young. Whether through our families of origin, movies, commercials or peer pressure, these standards can create something like the refrain a record player needle makes when stuck in its groove, playing over and over in your heart and head. It continually, for example, plays music with lyrics that say you are "not good enough." Often these standards are so ingrained that we have virtually no awareness of them—they are invisible. But we can see their reflection in how we feel in our lives and in some of the important choices we make. In fact, some standards make such a deep imprint that, even if we consciously decide that we no longer have to fulfill them, the self-criticism and self-rejecting feelings may linger for a long time. The feelings of pressure created by these standards and conditionings make for strong headwinds. Our friendly mind, with its friendly sensibility, counters these with simple wise guidance.

Here are nine of the most common areas where we are likely to be caught in some impossible standards that make activating friendly mind absolutely essential:

1. **Family:** This can have so many varieties that it is hard to compile a list. A few of them include feeling guilty for failing to satisfy a family member, feeling pressured to be different than you are in your life, or wanting to spend less or more time with a particular family member.

2. **Marriage and Having Children:** Attempting to live up to unrealistic, perfect expectations about what a wife or husband, or father or mother should be, or feeling pressure to fulfill the timing of when marriage or becoming a parent is supposed to happen.

3. **Success:** Feeling pressure to have a more successful career, lifestyle, or more money than is actually possible in your circumstances.

4. **Beauty/Body Type/Attractiveness:** Wanting to have an appearance that is not possible. Measuring yourself negatively for not being desirable enough.

5. **Youthfulness:** Expecting yourself to look significantly younger than you are or to have the physical capacities of a much younger person.

6. **Love Relationship:** Trying to achieve a quality of relationship that you think, correctly or not, others have—and blaming yourself or your partner when you haven't been able to, even though you've done all you believed was possible.

7. **Religion or Spirituality:** Feeling guilty for not following the tenets that you learned even when they don't really make sense to you. This could be sexually, morally or simply not following any of the traditions.

8. **Intelligence:** Feeling embarrassed and ashamed for what you perceive to be your limited intelligence in any area of your life, leading you to hide this from others.

9. **Confidence/Self-Esteem:** Feeling insecure and using that as a weapon against yourself.

If you identify with one or more of these situations, believe me, you are not alone. I know this feeling in my own life, and I have never worked with a client who doesn't bring some of these impossible or unrealistic standards into our sessions.

Our friendly mind matters so much to the improvement of the quality of our lives. This practice or way of supporting ourselves helps to free us from these impossible standards we've adopted from the outside often unknowingly. By exposing standards that prevent us from feeling good in our lives, friendly mind helps us to recognize the capacities and achievements that are within reach.

Reflection Point: What standard creates the greatest pressure on you to become a way that is not natural or possible now?

Taking It Deeper: If this pressure has created suffering for you, can your friendly mind help you address it? What might your friendly mind say?

Distinguishing Friendly Mind from Other Approaches that Claim to Support Well-Being

Our minds respond in challenging times in ways that might look like friendly mind—but once we look at what's happening more closely, we see that these ways are very different. There are four particular ones that

I've seen quite often that I want to share with you. It's important not to be hoodwinked by them! They are:

1. **Positive Thinking**
2. **Conventional Thinking**
3. **Negative Thinking**
4. **The Fixer Mentality**

1. Positive Thinking

One of the most beguiling of these is positive thinking—entertaining thoughts that you are hoping will have a beneficial effect. However, these thoughts are prone to being overly optimistic. Affirmations usually aren't grounded and don't deal with what you can actually do in a given situation or how you need to be to best take care of yourself.

What does positive thinking sound like? Here is a crystallized version of its many voices (there are infinite possibilities):

- I know I can find love if I just stay trusting myself.
- I am going to manifest the money I need just by staying focused.
- My fears are not based on what is real and I will be fine no matter what.
- I love myself unconditionally and I'm sure it will help.
- I wish everyone just realized it is their negative thinking that causes all of their problems. I am so happy because I haven't fallen into that trap.
- I believe I can do anything I put my mind to. Our minds are miraculous and if we steer them in the direction of believing everything will work out, then our lives will be the evidence of that.

While positive thinking may make life more optimistic, these kinds of thoughts usually don't address the necessary elements of development that are needed to really understand ourselves. Positive thinking doesn't often ask about the practical next steps to take to make it more likely to receive what we need the most. It's as if we all have a bit of Harry Potter inside us! We can wave our magic wand and it will be so. Another drawback of this positivity is that it frequently gets lost in generality or abstraction, never really addressing the reality at hand. There is also a danger these statements can become robotic and reduced to a distraction. To really support ourselves, we need to see what's actually in front of us in the present and look for and implement actions and attitudes that are realistically possible.

Conversely, friendly mind is based on the fact that you have made your realistic best efforts knowing that you deserve and trust in your friendly thoughts. Our best efforts do not mean they are *perfect* efforts, and we have to watch that we don't convert our friendly thoughts into yet another standard to meet.

2. Conventional Thinking

I would be a wealthy man if I had a quarter for every time I heard the response "I'm fine" or "I'm good," to the question "How are you doing?" For most people, even when in the midst of a challenge, this is their conventional reply—a blanket answer that makes it look like everything is fine even when it isn't.

This conventional approach to real pains and fears cuts off the empathy or help from others that could catalyze a better approach to the challenge. But for those of us who have a life that's working better than average, and which is relatively successful and peaceful, the conventional tendency is to compartmentalize the challenging aspects and emotions of our experiences.

Frequently, the rationale is "Why make a big deal out of it and burden yourself and others? What good is it going to do?" These questions may sound sensible but they have the effect of isolating us when we're hurting and frightened the most. There can be many reasons for this type of question. We may not want to be that transparent and vulnerable. Some of us have a view that we should be self-sufficient and that it would show a neediness or weakness to do otherwise. But whatever the reasons are, this view is a rationalization that leaves us isolated, and with no possibilities to reach out for help. Sure, some of us can work with our difficult feelings on our own, and sometimes that's the right decision. But just saying all is well causes us to miss sharing important opportunities for intimacy and relief, especially when we are with someone who might be able to offer caring in a sensitive and helpful way.

The voice of conventional thinking often sounds like this:

- I can take care of myself.
- I don't think there's any benefit to complaining.
- Nothing is going to help, so what's the point in talking about it?
- I feel invaded when others need to know what I'd rather keep private.
- I don't want the conversation to be so focused on me. I'd rather talk about something more interesting.
- It's an obsession to have to always talk about yourself.

Conventional thinking doesn't allow us to maximize benefit from sharing our vulnerability and giving and receiving on this deeper level. Friendly mind encourages us to share the challenges that we are facing with those that we trust the most. This deeper sharing is a prime benefit of our friendly mind. It allows us to have the best of both worlds: learning to be friendly and resourceful toward ourselves and giving and receiving from those we most trust.

Friendly mind is always looking carefully at the person you are talking with. And it has the capacity to be humble and courageous enough to acknowledge when times are tough. It wants to optimize your chances of being as fulfilled and healthy as possible, so it will encourage you to be open to all resources and anyone that might be of help. Your friendly mind is also happy to be self-sufficient when that is the best way to take care of yourself. Your friendly mind is not a fair-weather friend: it is always available to support you.

3. Negative Thinking

A more harmful substitute for friendly mind that often pretends to be your friend—but is just the opposite—is negative thinking. This voice claims with authority that it wants what's best for you, and it believes that it needs to keep telling you that you are not doing or being enough—to keep you alert. It believes it is trying to awaken you as it loudly tells you what you need to do, but it is actually critical and harsh. Most of us who have experienced this voice haven't been aware of how harmful its effects are. We believe the words and can't clearly see the rejecting and demeaning attitudes they contain.

What does this negative thinking sound like?

- I can't believe you still have this problem. Why don't you just do . . .
- I hate it when I feel this way. Let it go.
- I wish I could be more like . . .
- There's something wrong with me—I haven't been able to find a stable ability to love.
- Why do you act like you're the only one with a problem? It's embarrassing.
- You should be doing that and not this . . .
- You have to work harder than you do. The least you could do is admit that you have created your own problems.

As outrageous and crazy as it seems when you hear it, we often believe that overtly criticizing ourselves will make us better and can be a source of motivation. From observing my clients, myself, and those close to me, it is evident that many of us hold unconscious beliefs that being tough on ourselves will somehow make us stronger. Upon closer examination, however, it becomes clear that negative or critical thinking does not create motivation—it actually undermines our courage to change. We end up so demoralized that we gradually lose faith in ourselves.

We might say to ourselves, "I hate it when I feel so jealous," but then think, "At least I'm being honest with myself." Or we reject and resist our feelings only to find them magnified. Have you noticed what happens when you try to force your way out of a particular feeling? When you've been doing this, how has it been working out? Sooner or later, perhaps even now as you reflect on this, it becomes clear that you can best face your life's most difficult moments when you are accepted and encouraged.

We will explore the way negative thinking operates in greater detail in several later chapters, particularly when we turn to the subject of self-rejection.

Friendly mind gets the sorrowful hoax of trying to change ourselves through such negativity. It is very likely to ask you, "How often has it worked out well for you when you have berated yourself?" It is clear that friendly mind will steer you toward what will have a chance of making your life better, but will never do it in a negative way. Its methods are to use language that makes it clear that it is speaking to you with respectful, sensitive words. It can be strong if necessary, but never expresses itself with negativity. It asks you to do your best, but never in a way that puts you down.

4. The Fixer Mentality

The "fixer," often masquerading as the helper, is much more intellectually logical than the other ways of thinking. Its motto is: "Just fix it by either acting on something or denying anything needs to be done." The friends or loved ones who use this approach (more frequently men) often have an underground impatience with their own and others' feelings and propose ways to make the feelings go away. Most often they are sincere in trying to help, and simply don't realize what will bring benefit. If you are feeling sad, they are inclined to focus on what will cheer you up. If you are frustrated, they may guide you to just let it go because it's not going to do you any good. The difficulty is that the fixer doesn't realize that what can be most helpful is just to listen and care for the person who is feeling any type of challenge, so that person can either experience being loved as they are, or have time to reflect on how they can best take care of themselves.

What does this way of thinking sound like?

- How many times do I have to tell you that you are your own worst enemy and that if you just think about this rationally, you will feel better?
- The mind can solve any problem if you look at it from every angle and make a genuine effort.
- You do realize that you are reinforcing your pain by talking about it all the time, don't you? Just give it a rest.
- I hope by now you see what I've always been telling you: therapy is a bunch of crap, and all you need to do is not take yourself so seriously. It's really pretty simple.

Yes, the fixer can sometimes create a distraction or give the temporary illusion of changing difficult feelings, but their method is ineffective in creating support and it will ultimately injure intimacy.

Friendly mind doesn't sound like any of these four voices. It does not put out a "positive spin." Nor does it respond in a conventional way that leaves challenges unaddressed with the belief that we are fine. It also doesn't give everything—or for that matter anything—a "negative twist" under the guise of helping us to do better. And finally, it does not incessantly intrude into our awareness by claiming it will fix things and then fail to do so.

As I said earlier in the chapter, friendly mind is responsive to our reality in a grounded, supportive way—it is our best guide in the present. It is a thinker that steers us to engage our challenges with thoughts that are friendly and that contain simple caring wisdom.

Six Principles of Friendly Mind

Here is a closer look at this remarkably liberating way of thinking and supporting ourselves:

1. Being aware of present challenges

The first principle is simply letting yourself recognize and acknowledge that you are facing difficult times or circumstances in your life. You are honest about what they are and aware enough to be able to reflect consciously on them.

2. Thinking empathically when we feel stuck

Your friendly mind knows that you aren't feeling caught in any of your challenges or difficult emotions on purpose. It doesn't assign blame; it has empathic thoughts toward you and what you're feeling, even though when times are very difficult the empathy is likely to be only on a thinking level. It will say something like this to you:

- I'm sorry that you have to go through this and it is important to be a support to yourself. I am going to ask you some questions and will probably make some suggestions about how you can best take care of yourself when you can't change what you wish you could. Are you ready?

- Can you hear me and do you believe that it is important to listen to my response?
- I can hear that you aren't listening yet, and I will ask again and hope you hear me now.
- Remember this would be difficult for everyone. Just take a breath, in and out, and then consider what the next step is that you can take. It could be in your contemplation of how you can take care of yourself without having to change your feeling or the obstacle. By thinking simply and practically, you allow yourself to deal with what you're going through.
- And if you don't know, I will stay with you and remind you that not knowing means you are sincere and you need to keep asking as it will impact how well you care for yourself.
- Can you hear this? If not, we'll keep working this out together no matter how you feel. I can see how hard this is for you.

With persistence, you will eventually open up to the suggestions from your friendly mind. It's providing an important and different kind of empathy. Usually we associate empathy with feelings, but in many situations we may be suffering enough that our caring feelings aren't available to us. The best we can do during these times is to be empathic with our thoughts and our intellect. *We are following sensible <u>thoughts</u> rather than being controlled by disturbing feelings.*

Our simplest guiding friendly thoughts, then, are the ones we need to listen to, to be receptive to; otherwise, at these times, our lives will be consumed and directed by our disturbed feelings.

This kind of empathy for yourself is a communication between your friendly mind and your most challenging feelings. Your friendly mind is neutral as it encourages you to listen, helping you not to be frozen by your emotions. It has no interest in dominating or judging you, but simply wants to accept and relate to you as you are and then make its simple guiding suggestions.

3. Having friendly guiding thoughts without needing to feel friendly

Perhaps the hardest aspect of this principle is *accepting that sometimes we can't feel good no matter what we've tried to do.* Many of us, especially if we are under sixty years of age and may not have had much experience with serious health issues or mortality, have assumed that we can either feel good or virtually always find a way to get there. Friendly mind, however, understands that our immediate circumstances are sometimes unchangeable. In any given moment, it provides a crucial realism that relieves us from the pressure of our usually unconscious standards to reach a certain goal or to feel a certain way even when it is impossible.

We receive the most benefit from friendly mind if we can let go of needing to *feel friendly*, and allow a simple, thoughtful guidance to enter our internal safe and spacious zone. *The pressure to feel friendly inhibits the potential benefit of our friendly mind.* This pressure often makes us believe we're a failure for not feeling friendly. This is not helpful! We all need continuous reminders that having friendly thoughts is the best we can do at times when we are feeling our worst.

As I shared in the introduction, in my own life, those first years of contending with the unique effects of the kidney transplant medications were a personal hell. The medications created a humbling and dismal reality—I had virtually no access to my heart or sense of well-being.

In the blink of an eye or the ingestion of a pill, I was no longer the caring, empathic, relaxed person I had been. I made every effort I could conceive of, and along with the input of friends and teachers it became clear that there was nothing I could do to feel better except to be more accepting, neutral, and guide myself. Gradually I developed a capacity to have neutral guiding thoughts even while I felt horrible. I was learning that my self-worth or value was not predominantly based on my feelings. I began to be able to prioritize my friendly directing thoughts while my feelings of exhaustion and despair were still present. What a major difference this made in my life at that time—it was such a relief to know that when I felt the very worst, it wasn't necessary to feel anything positive. This knowing has become an integral part of my life. I felt relieved from the pressure to live up to my prior standards and baseline enjoyment of life. I experienced an inner knowing that nothing needed to change for me to be ok. With my natural best efforts, I could relax and let go without trying to figure out how it was going to be in the future.

4. Making our realistic best efforts for self-care

Don't make the mistake of thinking that friendly mind lets you "off the hook." Just because it is "friendly" does not mean you aren't accountable for how you are.

On the contrary, as I highlighted earlier, friendly mind is clear about wanting us to make our *realistic best efforts*. Each of these words matter. When I say "realistic best efforts," I mean a *sincere determination to apply ourselves to our situation—no matter how challenging it may be, and no matter what we may be feeling.*

I have learned a great deal from my clients about what realistic best efforts mean, particularly from those who have been faced with challenging medical circumstances.

Maria
After three spinal surgeries, Maria was feeling afraid, disoriented and hopeless. Even with the help of a walker, she could not walk for more than 200 steps—and every step was painful. In addition,

her doctors had put her on painkillers for the last nine months to deal with the impact of surgery. Maria was struggling with feelings that there was something wrong with her because she couldn't remember what had happened in the past and what was happening in the present. I reminded her repeatedly that the medications were creating the memory loss. The fear of having the experience of pain and the limitation in walking were things that were challenging her on a pretty consistent basis. The idea that they could be permanent was keeping her immersed in feelings of deep anxiety. We spoke numerous times about friendly mind—the part of her that was realistic, constructive, and wanting to deal with what was really possible for her rather than trying to control the future (which was totally impossible). She got the absurdity, humor and futility about continuing to stress over her uncontrollable future and over her inability to make herself feel deeply secure that she would be able to walk in a year.

As she activated her friendly mind, it reminded her that she was actually bringing her realistic best efforts, both practically and emotionally, to a terribly challenging situation. She was sharpening her focus on what she was capable of, which in her case often was literally how to take her next step, rather than trying to find a false security in a future hope.

5. Letting go of trying to solve the impossible

As the concept of realistic best efforts underscores, we ultimately need to accept what we cannot change. We cannot solve the impossible—not today, and perhaps never. Friendly mind does not expect us to be Superman or Superwoman. It supports us in being exactly who we are.

Not attempting to solve the impossible requires admitting that we can't successfully demand or force ourselves to change these states of core suffering. Perhaps you have seen that forcing yourself to try to feel different is not an effective strategy! Hopefully, this makes you smile at yourself as you see the absurdity of it. It is so helpful when we don't demand ourselves to be able to feel different than how we are. We can hear our friendly mind saying, *It is okay that you can't yet feel better in any way as you look closely and can't see any way to make it happen.*

On the following pages are two client case studies that help to illustrate this.

Jillian

Jillian had suffered from chronic anxiety throughout her life. It was not deeply disabling, but it was a fairly constant presence underneath whatever she was experiencing. She often had the thought that she and other people that she loved were in danger in ways that she admitted were unrealistic. Other times she felt insecure, and that she was going to be rejected because she believed her husband found her unattractive. This wasn't realistic either or based on the actual situation. Her anxiety caused her to feel overly concerned about the safety of her children and she felt that her relationship with her husband was genuinely unstable.

Her first inclination was to suppress or criticize herself for being "so ridiculously anxious." When I asked her, with a kind but ironic question, "Are you being anxious on purpose?" She smiled and said, "Of course not." She had tried all kinds of psychotherapy to relieve the anxiety but none of it really allowed her to address it in a way that restored her dignity and maximized her trust in herself. Over the next several months we explored the question: "Do you have any realistic way of getting rid of the anxiety in each situation as it arises?" As it became clearer and clearer that she didn't have a magic wand to make her anxiety go away, it became evident that her best option was to address it in the moment through the part of herself that was aware that she could direct kind and reassuring thoughts toward it. This was a way of both caring for it and being independent from it so she could carry on with her life.

Sometimes she would simply have an inner dialogue, such as "I'm sorry that you have to be anxious, but you can still give the very best love to others that you're capable of and be thinking empathically about the anxiety as well." Depending on the maturity and receptivity of the person that she was with, she shared a little about the anxiety.

Jillian was well on her way to practicing friendly mind when it mattered most: when she wasn't able to feel the way she wished she could. Her criteria of being her best self changed because she no longer had to get over her feelings. In fact, she recognized that she was even more proud and trusting toward herself when she could think in a self-caring way at these times.

Janice

After Janice suffered a stroke, she was very aware that she didn't speak nearly as well as before. Measuring herself against the standards of speech that she had developed before her stroke, she thought she should be able to speak "better"—more easily, more fluently and more articulately. After a difficult period of self judgment, she gradually learned to access her friendly mind. This led her to realize the obvious—that her standards were related to the past and no longer appropriate. They were completely unrealistic given her current circumstances.

She learned to focus on the present thoughts that she was trying to convey. When she wasn't able to find the words, she made it clear that she wanted others to keep asking her questions to help her articulate her meaning so that conversation became truly possible. She set up group meetings with people who had other disabilities so they could accompany and care for each other—she became the natural leader she was earlier in her life. Janice was no longer focused on the impossible goal of being able to talk as well as she could before the stroke. Thanks to her friendly mind, she gradually recognized that she was doing everything that she possibly could. Instead of judging herself harshly, she began to take pride in the progress she could actually achieve in being resilient in what was possible with her speech and her life.

In each of these situations, there is the desire to feel secure that things will get better and the deepening realization that this focus on the future causes endless fear and pain. By staying with the need to feel secure about a better present or future, it becomes impossible to be accepting and responsive in a way that is self-caring. This unrealistic exaggeration of a need becomes a desire for control and certainty that can never be attained. When we become aware of this exaggeration, we can naturally open to what is possible and our most natural and best self.

6. Focusing on the possible

We start with the awareness that we are pursuing something that is impossible, and that becomes the catalyst for grounding our friendly mind. This allows us to redirect our energy and attention to what is possible. So, instead of banging our heads against the wall, we increase the ways, large and small, to see and do what is realistic and how to best take care of ourselves.

In the case studies, the turning point for each of the three people was when they saw that they were reaching for completely impossible goals. As they learned to focus on the possible, they experienced a new dignity to their life's circumstances. This master key—listening to and moving from the impossible to the possible in the present and near future—allowed a new kind of strength and clarity. We experience a certain trust and peacefulness because we have confidence that we are skillfully facing the challenge at hand.

As you focus on the possible, you honor yourself for making your realistic best efforts. When you see the areas where you haven't made your best efforts, it is never too late to commit to being the best you can be next time. This builds trust in yourself—you can let the past go and feel more confident in your capacity to handle these challenges in the near future.

Here is a list of these six principles:
1. Being aware of present challenges
2. Thinking empathically when we feel stuck
3. Having friendly guiding thoughts without needing to feel friendly
4. Making our realistic best efforts for self-care
5. Letting go of trying to solve the impossible
6. Focusing on the possible

As these principles show, friendly mind never imposes ideas from outside of yourself. It is the part of yourself that sees from the perspective of what would be friendly and supportive toward you when the totality of your life is taken into consideration, and you've done all you can see that you can do. You may not be able to reliably hear what friendly mind is suggesting, but you *can* hear yourself *asking* what it would say to you at any given moment.

Even as you follow these principles closely, please remember: *friendly mind requires frequent self-reminders.* We often forget that we need to sustain our focus on how to support ourselves at the time we are most hurting, especially when we can't change something we wish we could. These self-reminders need to be played, mantra-like, in the background of our days.

Listening to the Voice of Your Friendly Mind

While the *sound* of our friendly mind's voice varies depending on the circumstances we are facing, it does have abiding *qualities*. It is either neutral or, when the challenges are not all consuming, it is supportive. To demonstrate this, here is the summary of a series of sessions in dialogue form, showing how friendly mind communicated with Jamie, who had been suffering from a melancholy state since he was a child. He had no shortage of good reasons for why he felt this way, as he had a very depressed mother, a lot of pressure to succeed from his father, and a broader family history of depression.

FRIENDLY MIND: I can see that you don't like feeling empty and melancholy—like most everyone else on the planet. What makes it so hard for you now?

JAMIE: I'm tired of having to deal with this so much of the time, and continuously having to experiment with a variety of medications.

FRIENDLY MIND: I know that you have been very diligent in your effort to find the right medications and to do whatever else is possible. This is by far the hardest time: when you're still actively looking and you haven't found anything that works. I'm really sorry that you have to go through this, but we both know you've done everything that you can do. Right?

JAMIE: Yes, but it sucks to feel this way.

FRIENDLY MIND: I can see how intolerable it feels to you. I encourage you to say, "Ok, emptiness, I can't change you now so I'm going to focus on what I *can* do."

JAMIE: I can see that that would be best, of course. It's just hard when the depression weighs me down.

FRIENDLY MIND: I recognize it's hard and that's why you want to say with as much authority as possible, "It's hard! I deserve to be kind to myself! I know it's the most difficult when I'm feeling down and I know I'm doing the best I can right now."

JAMIE: It seems like I keep forgetting.

FRIENDLY MIND: It's to be expected, when you've been suffering with something for your whole life, that you would need reminders to be patient and compassionate with yourself. Know that it's a mini-miracle every time you can: remember friendly thoughts when you're feeling down *and* be as present as possible.

This dialogue helped bring Jamie to the realization that he had unreasonable hopes and expectations that his chronic low-grade depression would finally leave him. His friendly mind then reminded him that the key was not to try to change his state, but to do his best to tolerate or accept it and then be as totally present with everything else that he was capable of at that point in time. As Jamie implied above, it wasn't easy, but he persevered, watched himself be able to feel down, be kind with his thoughts toward himself for feeling that way, and still be able to relate to his significant others in a way that showed he was present.

Jamie's emptiness is just one example of an infinite variety of challenges that each of us has. Hearing another's words may make it seem obvious what would be helpful; however, all of this isn't nearly as clear when we are dealing with our own challenges. As we look closely at our lives, most of us can see quite a number of times when we are being led by a reaction to an emotion or a thought that is not serving us or anyone else. In whatever unique challenge you find yourself in, when you can access your friendly mind, every little thought that is generated—no matter how small—is a great step.

Friendly mind is always encouraging us, asking:

> *Doesn't it seem to make sense to take the time to ask for my perspective, given these challenging feelings and situations you are facing? After all, I am only here to serve your well-being and not to harm you or anyone else. I'm not your mother, father or spouse. I am the friendliest voice that you have access to and I can provide you with immediate support. In a sense you could say I am the best "you."*

The voice of friendly mind simply and sensibly deals with what is possible rather than continuing to go for the impossible. It is pragmatic, unbiased, and even-tempered. As you activate it more and more, it will become the best, most sensible, and reliable voice you have ever heard.

▼

> **Reflection Point:** What words do you need to hear most now from your friendly mind? Let yourself look at one or two areas where you can open up to the help of some friendly words to guide you where you are most challenged emotionally.
>
> **Taking It Deeper:** What do you imagine a dialogue would sound like between your friendly mind and you regarding this challenge or feeling that you are facing?

Key Messages

Friendly mind exemplifies Einstein's famous realization that "We cannot solve our problems with the same level of thinking that created them." Although he was mainly speaking to a different level of life's mysteries, Einstein's understanding also applies to the way we face life's great challenges. We see that we cannot successfully work through the emotions in which we are embroiled at the same level of awareness that created them—we realize it's impossible to change our challenging feelings to better reach our heart through an act of will, but we know we <u>can</u> change our thoughts.

This is precisely why friendly mind can play such a pivotal role: it lifts us to a new level of awareness. As we have explored in this chapter, when we find ourselves frozen in an emotional impasse, it is our friendly mind that can shift our level of focus and guidance to support change and healing. It is a breakthrough every time we can do this.

Like strengthening a muscle with a workout at the gym, or sharpening our mind by studying for a test, using our friendly mind strengthens its potency and versatility. And the stronger it becomes, the more often we will rely on it. Over time, this "virtuous cycle" can transform our very lives. It will also enable a more effective use of the practices that follow.

Integrating the Chapter: Inquiries

- After reading this chapter, how much are you glimpsing your friendly mind? Or, are you aware of specific barriers to accessing it? If so, then take a moment to write them down so that you can do further work with them in the following chapters.
- What impossible standards might you still be holding onto? Congratulate yourself if you are aware of them and realize that this is where you'll need the most help with friendly mind.
- If your friendly mind has started to speak to you, how does the quality of its voice sound? Can you hear it clearly? If not, can you be a little friendlier with yourself in thought and realize that you are just getting started?
- As you identify the emotion or situation where your important desires are most out of control, can you hear your friendly mind speaking to you? If so, what is it saying and how does it sound?

For additional support and further integration of Practice Two, I strongly encourage you to listen to the guided meditations at www.AwarenessThatHeals.org.

Moving from Self-Rejection toward Self-Compassion

*It's a true insight when we can see how
our self-rejection undermines the potential
for our own compassionate heart to
respond to our pain.*

Whether we know it or not, some form of self-rejection is happening every time we do not care for ourselves just as we are. Deepening our awareness of the subtle and overt ways we reject ourselves is a major catalyst to moving us toward acceptance and self-compassion. We have so much to gain by becoming aware of this and cultivating awareness that heals when we are experiencing self-rejecting feelings or thoughts.

Take a look at any areas of your life where you feel anxious, judgmental, unfulfilled or inadequate—somehow just "not enough." How well do you care for these feelings when they occur? Do you automatically dislike them? Do you keep them held privately inside you? Are they hard to find? From all of the work I've done with myself and clients regarding that state of not being enough, I have found that, whether we recognize and dislike these feelings directly or abandon them inside, we are experiencing a form of self-rejection.

Most of us have the impression that we can easily see our self-rejection.

Some have a belief that it appears only when we talk negatively to or about ourselves. However, our inner critic is only a small part of the story: much of our self-rejection occurs on a more subtle level. Without a doubt, life provides situations that are difficult enough—causing feelings of sadness, helplessness, anger, frustration or other challenges. What makes it even worse is this extra layer that we rarely see or are even aware of, where we *feel* negatively toward ourselves for having pain, anxiety or anger in the first place. This hidden self-rejection accompanies almost any feeling that we perceive as suffering. I want to highlight here that *this type of self-rejection is one of the greatest sources of our long-term suffering and the most difficult to recognize.*

We are rejecting ourselves whenever we don't like how we are—and most of us have practiced this kind of self-rejection for so long that it's become virtually automatic and mostly exists outside of our awareness. *It would all be much easier if self-rejection stepped out into the open, but it often hides behind and underneath our more common day-to-day challenges.* It's a true insight when we can see how our self-rejection undermines the potential for our own compassionate heart to respond to our pain. When we can see this self-created wounding and activate our intention to reach our hearts, our self-rejection reveals itself. This gives us the opportunity to find ways to move toward kindness, trust and caring.

Just why do we fight against who we are and what we feel? And how can we heal, and be supportive of ourselves when we are in this fight? My body's unusual response to my kidney transplant medications left me only one good option: to explore these questions much more intensively. With hindsight, I can now see that in the beginning I was in a frequent state of self-rejection so subtle that, for a long while, I could not recognize it. During this period, deep down, I felt a sense of worthlessness: a reaction to my chemically induced anxiety, agitation, exhaustion and diminished vitality.

It was not only the effects of the medications that were upsetting me.

I was also upset because I wasn't able to reach the familiar inner essential qualities such as inspiration, love, gratitude and kindness that had naturally been part of my life before. It was only later that I became aware that I had been withdrawn because I couldn't accept and care for the changes induced by the medications.

Since that time, I have worked with many clients and friends who suffered in similar ways when they faced reduced capacity in any important area of their lives. And, of course, sooner or later this happens to us all. When we aren't what we used to be or don't live up to our own expectations, it is an almost universal reaction to not like ourselves in the ways we did before. Even when it's obvious that we have no control over, or responsibility for, the circumstances—such as an unavoidable health crisis—we still tend to reject ourselves. Our rejection can be expressed by withdrawal or by self-judgment directly. The common thread is that we invariably fail to recognize the rejection for what it is: a way of injuring ourselves that is outside of our awareness.

When we have a long-term or permanent loss, we often focus on the loss itself and miss seeing the underlying self-rejection that comes in the form of feeling failure, shame, withdrawal or a diminished sense of self-worth. Feeling and caring for ourselves at these times is an important capacity that most of us haven't developed or even thought about. Instead, we most frequently set impossible goals to regain the capacities that we've lost.

"I realize there is nothing I can do to change the effects the chemicals are having on my body," I once told a friend despondently soon after I first identified my self-rejection. This was at the stage when, even though I felt helpless to change my emotional states, I still thought I could do more. As my friendly mind evolved, I could see that what was happening wasn't emotional—it was a physiological state that depleted and lessened certain capacities. I could see my emotions were really an outdated response to these new conditions, and that that response was something I could work with over time.

My conversation with my friend evolved too. I could eventually speak in an even-keeled voice, following my intention to heal most of the time, no matter how I felt. I could see that the feelings about myself were rooted in unrealistic and impossible-to-achieve notions and, knowing that, I found a way to express what I truly believed in a new and important way. I began to find an antidote to the way I felt about my challenges—one that had the potential to significantly reduce or eliminate the extra layer of self-rejection I'd identified.

This friendly thinking came from a clear and good-natured place inside, rather than from the subtle disapproval, contraction and withdrawal connected to my self-rejection. The moment I understood that, I broke into tears, and I experienced my innocence and my longing to be kind toward myself. Something in me lifted, as this awareness was no longer subtle. It was the realization that I was still deserving and worthy of tenderness and caring toward my sorrow and my circumstances. Still, I virtually had no access to feeling the way I was used to, and in fact, no ability to feel almost any sense of well-being at all. This and several other similar realizations became a reference point from which I developed my friendly mind.

Discovering Self-Rejection: Key Questions

You can find out where you are rejecting yourself by asking these questions or similar ones:

- When I feel anxious and downcast, how much do I accept myself with kindness?
- How much empathy do I feel toward myself when I feel tight,

depressive, withdrawn or alienated?

- Can I embrace myself with warmth when I am feeling grief or terror?
- How much do I care for myself when I am feeling shame or guilt?
- How much support can I find in my heart for myself when I am angry or agitated?

When the answers to the above questions lean toward a "Not much," "No," or "None at all," then you are in some form of self-rejection. Questions such as these are beneficial in two ways: they give you the chance to open your heart in a softer and kinder way than ever before, and they are the best diagnostic tool you can use to enable you to discern when you are against yourself. As you ask yourself these questions, notice whether you welcome or resist them. Welcoming is a sign of openness to self-compassion. Resistance, and its negativity, indicate the strong likelihood of self-rejection.

In the following examples, you will see a challenging emotion and a self-rejecting feeling followed by a movement toward self-acceptance.

ANXIETY: EMBARRASSMENT AND INADEQUACY
I feel embarrassed and inadequate because of the amount of ongoing anxiety that I experience.

MOVING TOWARD SELF-ACCEPTANCE
I see that my anxiety has been part of my lifelong conditioning and I don't deserve to reject myself because of it. I know I'm not being anxious on purpose. I am developing trust that I can be both anxious *and* take care of whatever else is needed—including being devoted to my own kindness toward the anxiety.

ALONENESS: SHAME AND FAILURE

My wife and I had settled into a daily routine and it felt boring. I realized that neither of us was expressing an interest in how the other was doing, and it had created distance. I'm sure she was feeling the same thing. I was ashamed and felt like a failure because I had not had a substantial conversation with her as to how we could both be more satisfied.

MOVING TOWARD SELF-ACCEPTANCE

I saw that I needed to summon the courage and humility to talk about how I felt. I was ready to ask for what I needed, and invited her to express her needs too. I could feel a wave of relief and ease with myself.

SHAME: FRAUDULENCE

I feel my insecurity and a sense of personal fraudulence and deep shame as I distort and exaggerate the depth of knowledge I have to impress others. I constantly emphasize how close I am to "important people."

MOVING TOWARD SELF-ACCEPTANCE

I am now aware of feeling insecure and see that I was overcompensating by trying to impress other people. I am going to talk with a close and trusted friend about the last time I did this. I think this will allow me to develop a deeper trust in myself.

WITHDRAWAL: EDGINESS

I recognize that often I can't feel my heart being open, and at these times I am edgy or withdrawn. I feel stuck in resistant and disturbing emotions. In short, I've shut down emotionally. I hate to feel so closed and tight, but I haven't been successful at doing anything about it. It keeps going on and on. I don't like that I hide these feelings—from everyone else, and frequently from myself.

MOVING TOWARD SELF-ACCEPTANCE

I can see how it's really difficult for all of us to reliably open our hearts. I feel a growing tolerance toward myself as I let in the understanding that it is common for people to withdraw and be uptight. I'm appreciating how much more honest and accepting I am becoming and want to be. I'm gathering the courage to share with close friends how much I'm working to open my heart and allow them to support me while I'm struggling.

The intent of these examples is to help you open new doors toward awareness that heals. Gaining insight into your self-rejection is actually a cause for celebration. Why? *Because you have given yourself a chance to support your heart to expand,* as opposed to remaining stuck in a recurring pattern of rejecting yourself because of your reactions to your own suffering. This positive response to uncovering your self-rejection and seeking increased self-compassion is very important because it inspires you to feel safe as you look very closely at yourself with greater acceptance and kindness.

Reflection Point: As you read the previous examples, did they bring to the forefront any of your own patterns of self-rejection? Can you see any situations in your life where you might be rejecting yourself for an attitude, feeling or behavior that you don't approve of? What words, actions or qualities would help to guide you toward healing instead of using old patterns against yourself?

Taking It Deeper: Can you identify any feelings or actions that you don't feel good about? These may feel more like body sensations, such as contraction, upset stomach or feeling shaky. If you can identify these feelings or sensations—which may be fleeting—what caring words do you want to start to focus on that would be most soothing or empowering as you deal with the challenge you're experiencing?

Exploring the Origins of Self-Rejection

Given that we have so much to gain by developing self-acceptance and compassion, why do we continue to respond in a way that is against ourselves? What causes self-rejection in the first place?

Most parents modeled what they considered right and wrong through their behaviors, words, energy, tone and other actions. Sometimes this supported our lives, and at other times we were left wounded or feeling like we failed. Our broader cultural conditioning that steadily set many unreachable ideals also influenced us. What we were exposed to was likely done without intent or awareness.

Our upbringing and society have created so many unconscious goals and ideals that we all are basically set up to fail. Whether we want to fulfill them or rebel against them, either way we can't win. Inevitably we are led to feel a sense of failure or self-rejection. One of the most common and widespread examples is how we learned from those around us which gender-specific emotions were acceptable. The classically recognized standards were boys shouldn't act vulnerably or cry and girls shouldn't be angry or strong. We learned—mainly from our parents, our relatives and our teachers—which emotions, out of a vast range, we would be rejected for and which ones we would be accepted and praised for. We were also taught, as explored earlier, how we should succeed, how important our appearance is, how and when we should get married, when we should have children, what views we should or shouldn't have about religion, sex, and so much more.

As I mentioned earlier, most of us were taught that we needed to appear to have it "together" when we are with others. If we are anxious during these times, this will lead not only to suffering from the anxiety itself, but also to rejecting ourselves because we are embarrassed that we are anxious. It may be that the body chemistry we were born with or early life wounding is the cause of our anxiety. This anxiety may or may not be changeable, but we are likely to continue to reject ourselves and experience shame just for feeling it. Most of us, having no knowledge that there are other ways to care for the anxiety, are led into a futile cycle of denying, rejecting or suppressing it. This doesn't work out well, because it doesn't allow us the opportunity to be in contact with healing qualities and actions.

Our hidden self-rejection contributes to so much of our pain. Unless we become aware of it, we remain unable to heal and genuinely care for ourselves. Self-rejection is one of the main barriers preventing us from reaching the depth of our hearts—the place where kindness, tenderness and acceptance reside within each of us. When we have more access to the qualities of our heart, we can more easily care for the more challenging parts of ourselves.

The Journey toward Self-Acceptance

Every time you're aware of rejecting yourself for any reason, it is time to focus on accessing your intention to support yourself. This will take you further along your unique path toward self-acceptance.

Jeremy

Jeremy came to me in an agonized state of self-hatred for what he experienced as despicable feelings of anxiety and agitation. It was painful for me to see anyone give themselves such a hard time. He had no mercy. As we worked together, he courageously faced the reality that he had inherited a chemical imbalance from one of his parents and had a depressive anxiety condition.

With this awareness and a heroic amount of time dedicated to developing his intention to heal, Jeremy was able to gradually dis-identify with the illusion that these feelings were who he was. He was able to access his friendly mind more and more easily. This didn't mean that his anxiety disappeared.

However, his response to his anxiety, aided by his friendly mind, helped him to relax more with himself and know that he was not defined by his anxiety. He was able to say from the point of view of his awareness that heals, "I realize how hard this is for me just to maintain my inner equilibrium. I'm sending myself a message of trust and respect for my hard work of responding independently of my anxiety and accepting that it is there with no malice or intent to do something wrong. I know I may not be able to feel this, but I know I deserve this kindness." He knew he was worthy of love, and because of this, his self-rejection steadily decreased.

"I am not so consumed by how anxious I feel now," Jeremy told me. "I care about how I respond. I trust myself now to know what I need to do."

From everyday situations to ones where there is some sustained kind of loss of capacity, or illness, physical pain or physiological imbalance, being able to listen to your friendly mind instead of your temporarily out-of-control self-rejection is truly an act of self-compassion. It beckons us with: "You may not be able to feel this yet, but staying with it will increase the chances you will."

When we are aware of our self-rejection, it can reveal the potential healing that is hidden behind it: self-acceptance and self-compassion. When you notice that you are rejecting yourself or even just feeling bad for how you have expressed yourself, it is so helpful to continue to explore and contemplate how to move toward acceptance and appreciation of yourself.

It is important to look closely at what I mean by "self-acceptance." For many it means only the attitude we have toward ourselves—and not toward those that we are affecting. I believe this is a classic misunderstanding of acceptance; it is demonstrated when we say anything like, "I accept myself for my need to express my authentic anger toward my wife, so I really let her have it." We might feel accepting toward the release of our anger, but, as is the case with any essential quality, it matters if we are creating harm toward those around us. We need to be careful not to justify our feelings and their expression. Acceptance as I am using it means that we are not creating harm to anyone that can be avoided. Of course, there will be situations where others might be hurt by what we say. It is important that we make the distinction between harm that is due to our insensitivity versus the unavoidable hurt that can be created even when we express ourselves with as much sensitivity and thoughtfulness as possible.

When we ask whether we can accept and feel supportive of ourselves when we are afraid, we will most likely feel confused and say, "No." This is because we believe that opening our hearts to our suffering means that we are condoning, approving or encouraging it. This is a gross misunderstanding. *The truth is that whenever we accept, love, and open our hearts, it will allow us to find our way to optimally heal. Instead of keeping us stuck in our feelings, it becomes a way to enable us to be freer and freer.*

When we exacerbate the challenging situation by rejecting ourselves, we keep ourselves one step further from healthy independence. We can experience self-rejection in many forms: the following scenarios demonstrate some of these; they also show different forms of self-acceptance.

1. We may feel like a failure for never achieving our financial goals—realistic or not. And then, underneath this, we can contract and be agitated toward our sense of failure as we reject ourselves. Instead of remaining lost in this contraction and rejection, we can ask, "How can I best support myself by doing everything I can that is realistically possible?" Asking this question and persevering with it will both support us to stay grounded in making our best efforts and help us toward acceptance and self-caring. We can then naturally say to ourselves, "I like how you are making this effort."

2. We can be tormented by a fear that we are no longer attractive to

our partner. We feel too afraid and vulnerable to even ask how our partner feels or check it out—we are paralyzed and hyper-focused on our appearance. We carry the shame of being consumed by our fear, which is a form of self-rejection. If we can stay aware of the shame, and find our intention to care for ourselves, we can use it to move toward making the best of our appearance and cultivating acceptance and self-compassion. Often our fear has nothing to do with our partner or even an objective view of our appearance. It can be solely low self-esteem that we need to work on.

3. An addicted family member acts in ways that we see they are hurting themselves. We feel angry and upset that they're putting themselves in jeopardy. We want to scream at them to wake up. Having tried and failed to help them with their addictive behaviors including therapy and treatment facilities, we are totally exasperated. We hate feeling this way. Underneath, along with our anger and concern, we feel guilty for the times we have been insensitive and negatively reactive. When we stay aware of our guilt and find our wish to move toward healing, we naturally look for a way to be at least harmless and not add to their suffering in our effort to help. We can say to ourselves, "I appreciate how resourceful I've been and how hard I've tried. I will keep looking for ways to be helpful and avoid making things worse. I am going to apologize from my heart for the times when I have expressed myself with negativity because I know this didn't express my real intention."

These three situations, and many more you could imagine or have experienced, are hard in themselves. When we add pressure or self-judgment, it is certainly not helpful. What *is* helpful is becoming aware of our self-rejection and allowing this to catalyze a movement in us toward self-caring and acceptance. Whenever we succeed in being aware of our self-rejection and shifting the focus, we've achieved a major turning point in opening our hearts both to ourselves and those around us.

Identifying Self-Rejection in Relationships

For many of us, it is in the area of love relationships that there is a significant amount of self-rejection. This is not surprising because it's where the need for acceptance—of ourselves and from our partner—is usually the greatest.

Cynthia

After not seeing my long-term clients Cynthia and Thomas for many months, Cynthia came in one afternoon to tell me that she was considering going on anti-depressants. A successful real estate developer, she said she'd been depressed for the last few months.

"Do you know what triggered it?" I asked her.

"When I spend time with the kids, I get overwhelmed and I have to constantly leave the room and take breaks," she told me. "I just can't take them for too long."

Ten days before, Thomas had said to her, "I don't understand why you always need so many breaks, Cynthia. You already have plenty of help around the house from our nanny."

Internally, she had agreed with him that she was failing badly, and that there was something wrong with her. "Why can't I love more?" she asked.

Cynthia looked devastated when she explained to me that when she spent more than a few hours at a time with her kids and Thomas, she usually got depressed. She was judging herself very harshly for wanting to get away from her family.

When I encouraged her to look at what caused the depression, she realized that she felt claustrophobic. She had no way to regain her equilibrium when she got home from the few hours a day that she worked and she hated herself for that. "Why can't I just be like all the other wives and mothers I know who derive great satisfaction from being with their families?" she asked with tears in her eyes. She felt like she was failing her family.

"You're not even close to being a bad mom," I reassured her, adding that I had observed her sensitivity—even in tough times—myself, and heard the same from all of her family members. "You're not failing or abandoning your family. This is not about being good or bad. It sounds to me like you're rejecting yourself for needing more frequent breaks. You know, your particular nervous system can't help you to stay centered for eight hours at a time. Given the wounds from your alcoholic mother's vacillation between neglect and smothering that you experienced as a child, you can expect you will be exhausted and struggling for space. Because of this, you have had to reinvent yourself as a mom. The best you can do at first is what you have done—you've worked hard to be harmless.

There are some women who are naturally wired to be 24/7 moms and others who have to summon up their energy with will and take occasional breaks. You need to give yourself time and space to regenerate. You need a sanctuary, your own private space where you can be silent, breathe, meditate and reach for your heart."

As tears of relief came to her eyes, Cynthia relaxed.

"The question here," I continued, "is not whether it's okay to want a sanctuary for yourself. It's more than okay. It's essential. The real question is 'Are you kind enough to give it to yourself?'"

Cynthia smiled as she recognized and began to release the self-rejection that had caused her depression and shame. She had not been aware that she was rejecting herself. She thought she was simply depressed and inadequate. For some time after our session, she knew that she was really doing her best and yet still couldn't feel for herself. She wasn't able to feel a kindness toward her own dilemma. This was a time where she relied on her friendly mind to say, "You know you have worked your ass off with this more than anything you have ever done." Cynthia did what she needed to do for herself, and near the end of the year she experienced significant relief from her depression.

Cynthia was in a fortunate position to give herself the healthy space she needed. Many other mothers in a similar situation to Cynthia's don't have that luxury. In their case, they would need to cultivate self-compassion in order to soothe themselves at the source of their suffering. They would need to guide themselves with statements like, "I am doing the very best I can, and it is natural to be exhausted," or "I need to take as many naps as possible," or "There are millions of other mothers that are tired like me and it is heroic to be so devoted," or "My own lack of mothering has made it so hard that I need to be as gentle as possible with myself."

In situations like these, opening to self-rejection can help us gradually move from feelings of inadequacy and shame toward greater confidence and self-acceptance. And when we know we are on the road to having greater trust in ourselves, and see that we still don't know how to gain it, we can find ourselves facing a dilemma. At this point, many of us are usually discouraged because we can't see the path in front of us and this often creates a tendency to withdraw. It's exactly when we aren't feeling the good feeling we are seeking that we need to find encouragement to continue. This is also the time that our friendly mind is the ideal guide, because it is natural for friendly mind to acknowledge that we have been doing the best we know how to so far, and that we deserve to be supported to stay engaged.

From my work in relationships, another common pattern I have observed that leads to self-rejection is when one partner is more insecure than the other. This can be conscious or unconscious. The partner who feels insecure almost always dislikes this trait within themselves. They are often concerned that if they let their partner know about it or face it themselves, it will make things worse and put the relationship in jeopardy. If you identify with this, even in a small way, the following story may benefit you or your partner.

John

A client of mine, John, had lived with his insecurity so long that he assumed it was a permanent state. He became resigned to it, and felt hopeless to change it. I encouraged him to bring his awareness to it, and see if he could find an intention to heal so he could begin to work with himself in a constructive way. As John attempted this, he noticed that he just didn't know how to make himself feel more secure. But instead of rejecting the insecurity, he started to ask how he could take care of it or at least be with it without turning away. I encouraged him to enter into an internal dialogue and ask questions like, "How can I help myself become more secure?" "What specific areas of growth do I need to focus on to develop confidence?" "What actions do I need to take in order to feel more secure?" When he sincerely asked these questions, they led to other questions and even included his partner in some cases. His inner response led him to see he needed to improve his communication skills both in expressing his needs and listening to those of his partner. His answers also led him to develop more discipline in taking care of his body, and an ability to be more empathic to his partner's experience. He couldn't help but be encouraged to feel more trust and confidence in himself as he continued to grow in these ways.

Strategies to Disempower Self-Rejection

As you become aware of self-rejection and its judgments, it can be helpful to imagine yourself as the defendant in a courtroom. But there is no judge or defense attorney, only a relentless prosecutor—in this case, yourself!! The following strategy is particularly powerful to use when you know you are in a situation that you can't change, yet you continue to reject yourself nonetheless. When you can see that you are more innocent than your self-judgment makes you out to be, it's much easier to stand behind and support yourself.

I encourage you to repeat these three steps often enough so that they become second nature:

1. You are aware that you are condemning yourself and that the judgments that you are laying on yourself are not accurate or beneficial in any way.

2. You have a deep motivation to support yourself and recognize that you have a growing conviction to protect and defend yourself with strength.

3. You practice until you can express clearly and passionately your words of truth, directing them toward your distorted and destructive judgments.

As you determine that the self-rejection is based on false and unbeneficial self-judgments that have no real possibility of leading to healthy change, you can gradually gain the strength to stand up to this rejecting part of yourself, and say with growing conviction, "STOP! You're unfair and judgmental! These thoughts aren't the truth, they're not real and will not lead me to any healthy changes. I want you to know that I am from now on devoting myself to telling you that I am doing my best whenever I am. Give me a chance to change *in concrete ways* or I will know without a doubt that you and your judgments are only interested in hurting me. If you really don't give me options then I'm going to tell you to **get lost**!" You will likely have to go through many rounds with yourself, but at least you are now clear about who you can be.

It can take time to gain the strength to use statements of this nature, but it is very much worth the effort. It is so counterproductive when we reject ourselves for something that we can't change—especially if it is hurtful to us—and we are aware of it.

Most of us don't know how to be our own defense attorney or advocate and we need to grow into this capacity. We are being controlled by self-rejection in areas that are rooted in repeating others' judgments inside ourselves—ones we don't agree with. This growing strength will need the help of our friendly mind. We can't expect ourselves overnight to be as strong as the vilest judgments against ourselves. Just knowing that we are speaking the truth to ourselves will naturally grow in conviction with practice. We need to keep our awareness focused on our wish to move toward healing, and stand behind the truth of what we truly believe, no matter how long it takes.

Another strategy that is useful in helping us see our self-rejection more clearly is to playfully exaggerate or idolize our self-criticism. This can reveal the absurdity of how brutal we can be toward ourselves, and with that, we can begin to have an inner conversation with less self-rejecting dialogue.

If you realize that you have accused yourself of being worthless, you might say to yourself in an exaggerated tone, "Yes, I am completely worthless and everybody, from the person I passed in the street this morning, to the cashier at Costco, to my mother—everybody knows it!" Of course, you would say this with a smile and with humor. It is a way of showing yourself how absurd it is to think the criticism could be in any way beneficial—and you can hopefully have a good laugh about it while you're at it!

When Self-Rejection Contains Healing Messages

When we access our awareness that heals, we are able to see that some of the messages that come with our self-rejection can be constructive and important ones for our growth in spite of how harmful they feel or how they are presented. To discriminate, we need to develop both our capacity to be receptive and our ability to separate the essential message or potential truth from the "negativity" in the delivery. The most important question we can ask ourselves when we are confronted with negative energy that contains some truth is: "What is the message that I need to listen to so that I can grow or be more fulfilled?" Can we have the courage to look at how to best challenge ourselves in a healthy and constructive way—not through pressure or negativity, but through the inspiration of a potentially helpful insight about ourselves? Basically, we want to look objectively and honestly at what we're hearing without disqualifying it out of hand because of how it is presented.

You may say critically, "It's obvious that I'm withdrawn and avoidant of sharing my needs and that this is really self-destructive." Sarcastically you say to yourself, "Do you expect others to be psychic?" You might see that this judgment isn't helping you because it is punishing, but you see that it also contains the message that you are not expressing needs—and that is true. You then might say to yourself, "I am going to explore new ways to express my needs as sensitively and directly as possible. I'm also going to be careful from now on to notice that, when I judge myself, I get zero benefit out of it! I'm committed to finding the potential truth and throw out the rest of the judgments—they aren't helpful!"

Another judgment you might hear from yourself is "My strong emotions create too many demands on myself and those around me." Again, you may see that it is true that you want to stop having a critical attitude toward yourself and yet, at the same time, you see that you want to guide yourself to take care of certain emotions in ways that create more peace and intimacy. You would still want to develop the strength to deal with the harmful judgments directed toward yourself, but be able to stay open to find ways to care for yourself even when your energy is volatile and negative.

▼

Reflection Point: Of all the ways that you have judged yourself or been judged, can you see anything you've avoided that you still need to learn? As you think about it, let yourself say as strongly as you can, "I reject the energy that this judgment is being conveyed with, but I am still open to learning from any insight that it is showing me."

Taking It Deeper: In your love relationship, can you see places where you have an important healing message to deliver but get caught in delivering it in a judgmental tone?

Coping with Medical and Chemical Impacts

As I've mentioned before, there are many sources of emotional challenge that are beyond our control. And as my own experience indicates, medical and/or chemical crises can sometimes be the most challenging of all. At these difficult times, it is important that we support our awareness that heals and self-acceptance. Seeing clearly that we can't control some of these elements of life makes it easier to feel worthy of care and compassion when we're in the midst of these challenges.

Illness is a fact of life, and it can occur at any age. We may have chronic pain. We may have capacities that are diminished and certainly will be if we are fortunate enough to grow old. Some of us may have inherited issues with chemistry or DNA imbalances. All these issues can lead to feelings of rejection or inadequacy. Intellectually we may understand these conditions are not our fault, but we may still feel that something is wrong with us. And yes, there is something physically wrong, but what I am referring to here is that at these times, we are also prone to feeling that there is something wrong with us emotionally, too, and that we don't deserve to be loved because of it. This also includes natural conditions in life cycles such as PMS or other hormonal mood shifts which occur in both sexes. Even though rationally we know we don't deserve blame, we can often feel elements of shame or self-rejection. And, of course, this applies to others we know, too.

But being sick is one of the most common, and inevitable, areas where self-rejection has debilitating effects on our lives, and in turn impacts the ones we love. This is rarely understood and it is crucial to integrate it as we seek to support ourselves, and others, especially when we're facing moderate or serious pain, illness or mortality. If you've been fortunate enough to have consistent good health, you may not have thought very much about this.

The primary way self-rejection appears in this context is that we feel, in an irrational and exaggerated way, that we are a burden on others. We may also experience ourselves as a failure, which can result in withdrawal, isolation or anger on top of the challenge of the illness itself. This frequently leads to a very subtle feeling of worthlessness (which is deepened by feelings of rejection) that is often misinterpreted, by ourselves and our family, as being due to the illness itself. This misinterpretation is very hard to see, as I learned so clearly with my own responses to the chemicals I needed for my kidney transplant.

Helene

A friend, Helene, told me about her experience of attending a seminar with meditation teacher and death and dying expert Stephen Levine. She was animated when she said, "Robert, I have to share this with you because Stephen believes what you've been telling me for a long time." She told me how the room was full of young people with AIDS and cancer. Many of them were suffering deeply. Stephen stood up to address everyone. In a calm and tender tone of voice, he asked, "Who believes that we create our own reality?"

A large show of hands went up. Stephen looked at his audience and said, "That is one of those half-truths that can be extremely dangerous. All of us will have times when we have no control over choices about what happens to our bodies when we are ill. The only choices we have are how we go through the experience." Helene told me that a visible wave of relief flowed through everyone there.

After Helene told me this, and after feeling my appreciation for Stephen's work and what he said, I thought about friendly mind. I would have liked to have spoken about it with Stephen's audience. Speaking for friendly mind, and addressing their guilt and shame, I would have said something like, "Are you kidding me? Show me the person anytime in history who went through this kind of experience and *didn't* feel it was difficult." I might have suggested they say to themselves, "Even though I can't feel it now, I do realize I deserve mercy and caring. It is outrageous that not only am I immobilized physically by this condition, but I also am giving myself a hard time over it. I am going to bring this awareness to my intention to care for myself and be friendlier in my thinking. I know I deserve self-compassion and friendliness even if I can't feel it."

The idea that we are fully responsible for our illness or dying can lead us again to a reaction of feeling like a failure or even more of a burden. This is an unnecessary cruelty when we are already being challenged so severely. I flashed on several clients' and friends' parents that I had been with that were dying or very sick and on the conversations about how challenging it was to be facing and experiencing loss of capacity and possible death. So many people felt relieved to feel deserving of love, from others and for themselves, while facing these conditions.

Sometimes I will ask a client in a gentle tone, "Do you feel lovable while you are feeling this sick?" Often, it is the first time someone has ever asked them this question or one like it. And sometimes they say, "How can you ask me if I feel lovable when my body is in such bad shape, when I'm feeling so weak?" Most often, I will say something like, "I feel we all deserve love and mercy at a time like this." The truth is that the state of our physical body doesn't have to dominate our self-love. And almost all of us also need the support of good friends, family or a therapist when we are feeling very sick.

Fred

I was with a group of male friends a short time ago, and one of them, Fred, began talking about his challenging health condition. He loved playing golf and he was chastising himself for not being able to play as well as he used to. He said it had nothing to do with his medical condition, but we all knew that Fred had been substantially physically weaker since his illness. After all, he had lost fifty pounds and he had been hardly overweight to begin with. At this point he had just gotten through his twelfth round of radiation.

Caringly I said to him, "Do you realize that your conditions have changed? Are you really saying that your radiation and weight loss have nothing to do with how far you can hit a golf ball?"

Everyone laughed warmly. Fred suddenly saw the absurdity and he chuckled out loud, too. He clearly understood, for the first time since he'd gotten sick, that he was rejecting himself for something he couldn't possibly change. Sometimes humor is the best way to experience acceptance. Here, it allowed him to open himself to his friendly mind with playful statements like, "I guess maybe radiation *has* affected my capacity to hit the ball the way I did. I do deserve a break." It is amazing to see the relief that comes right on the heels of supportive thoughts.

Alan

My experience with Alan was similar in nature. I worked with him when he was dying. Before we talked, he had automatically assumed with fleeting awareness that he was a burden and useless to the people around him because of his deterioration. He wasn't very conscious of feeling that way until we talked it through. When I asked him, "Isn't feeling useless and burdensome almost as difficult as dying?" he immediately started to cry with feelings of self-compassion. He was so grateful to have someone to share his feelings with, rather than just being alone with them.

He could then focus on how he could feel most useful or

most connected while he was dying. This question enabled him to stay more caringly present—not only with his own pain but also with his kids and his wife. He would say to himself with his friendly mind, "I can understand why you feel less useful," and he would acknowledge his feelings, while simultaneously finding ways to connect with his family and still be the father that he wanted to be. Recognizing and caring for his self-rejection and bringing his intention to heal to those around him in little ways gave him honor and dignity while he was dying. It was so relieving to him to become more fully aware of his feelings of burdensomeness and failure and then to counteract that and reach toward merciful kindness and engagement.

Fred and Alan benefited immensely from their friendly minds. While we can't just magically change our conditions, or at times our feelings, we can learn to develop a friendly mind to guide us to have the best chance to increase our potential to have an impact on how we feel about our circumstances.

Making Confusion Your Ally

One of the times that we most often reject ourselves is when we feel confused about something important. We may start out on a given day feeling empty or somber, and we may not be able to understand why we feel this way as we scan our life. On another day, we might feel unsure as to how we can bridge a gap in our love relationship. The resulting confusion is very uncomfortable and leaves us with feelings of aloneness and alienation.

If you recall the last time you felt any of these or similar feelings, and they resulted in a state of confusion, chances are you had a knee-jerk reaction and you either pushed the confusion away in frustration and helplessness or felt intolerant, thinking, "I can't stand feeling so helpless." For many of us, especially at times when we are confused while facing and not suppressing a significant issue, it feels as though an electric current is buzzing through our nervous system, short-circuiting us with agitation. Our ego likes to believe it understands and the "need to know, feel good or fix ourselves" can border on neurotic inside us. Our urgency to be clear and sure is so strong because we often can't tolerate the suffering of feeling lost or helpless. This has caused confusion to become a kind of a taboo and most of us either reject it very soon after it arises or become downcast or withdrawn.

The good news is that confusion can be a powerful ally. We can make it ours if we allow ourselves the space to feel it and give it the reverence and respect that it deserves. We can't grow unless we stretch deeply enough inside ourselves to find the areas where we are unclear. If you look back at the big breakthroughs in your life, and think about how you felt, wasn't awareness of confusion very often an essential initial stage that led to change?

To simplify: *our problem is not the confusion itself, but the rejection of our confusion.* This rejection is frequently rooted in the unconscious belief that "I have failed because I don't know something," or "I am never going to figure out how to solve the problem," bringing with it all the accompanying unwanted feelings of deficiency such as self-doubt, helplessness and hopelessness. If we bring awareness that heals to this challenge, then, instead of going into doubt and withdrawal, we will naturally support ourselves to keep looking for the direction we need to take in the midst of the confusion and relax more with it. Awareness that heals will increase our patience and trust to be with the confusion as something important, and it may even inspire encouraging comments like, "I know it's hard to stay relaxed, but haven't we already seen that major breakthroughs come from exploring confusion and things you don't know how to solve?" This is a move toward self-acceptance.

When you are experiencing confusion, here are some statements you could contemplate:

- I can let in the knowing that my confusion is sincere and worthy of respect and persevering curiosity.
- I can feel the wisdom in understanding that this confusion is a signal to me that there is a need to find awareness … and this has the capacity to liberate me.
- I respect that confusion is part of the universal condition that all of us live in from time to time, and it deserves my deep appreciation and respectful attention.
- I can see that investigating confusion is a necessity for me if I want to live life in a more inspired and fulfilled way.

Key Messages

Many of us have seen self–compassion as something that is part of having a warm-hearted relationship with ourselves. At first glance, it doesn't seem like it should be hard to be kind to ourselves. But as we have seen, this is a very idealistic view as there are so many elements of hidden self-rejection that need to be uncovered and engaged with sensitivity and awareness.

We first need to recognize and become aware that virtually all of us have areas we dislike about ourselves that we can't see clearly. We need to ask, "Where is this most prevalent in my life?" and be prepared to say, "Oh good, I can see more clearly where I am giving myself a really hard time." (Hopefully this makes you smile or sigh with relief.) This response changes what normally leads to more rejection and isolation into a treasure waiting to be discovered. Only when we realize that we not only suffer, but also react negatively to the suffering itself, do we increase our chances to really use this awareness and move toward our intention to care for ourselves. It is the turning point: we see we are in the middle of disliking ourselves and shift to become more supportive.

This is a mini-miracle every time it happens as we begin to access a deeper level of self-acceptance and self-compassion. We can't bypass the critical stage of rejection. *It is utterly paradoxical in that the key to self-compassion is caring for our self-rejection.* It is a heartening expansion when we actually want to ask ourselves, "Anywhere else you don't like yourself that you can see?" This takes courage at first but once we see this awareness and understanding as our gateway to self-compassion, it becomes easier and easier.

Once we realize that we want to care for ourselves when we may have ignored or rejected ourselves, we will need the help of our friendly mind. It will tell us, "This may be hard to face; it's been there a long time. But congratulations for staying more and more with how you can, with patience, move toward healing and self-acceptance. You can't expect the changes in feeling to happen immediately, but hang in there because you are on your way to uniting with yourself in the most profound and rewarding ways that are possible."

I hope you feel encouraged that you can find your areas of self-rejection more easily now, and are motivated to bring them out in the open and care for them. The benefits are immeasurable, and the risks are very low when you develop a friendly mind and an intention to heal.

Integrating the Chapter: Inquiries

1. What are the most obvious feelings or situations around which you have a critical attitude toward yourself?

2. How much are you in touch with an intention to heal or a wish to cultivate greater kindness in these areas?

3. What question can you ask yourself to help you discover if you are caring or empathic when your challenges arise? Write down the thoughts and actions that you would like to adopt in order to move toward healing when you can see that you are rejecting yourself.

4. As you look at your most difficult thoughts or feelings of self rejection (e.g., shame, guilt, judgment), what is the one quality that you want to develop to experience deeper self-care (e.g., kindness, tolerance, acceptance, sweetness)? If you are having difficulty identifying the specific quality that you need, the **Introspective Guides** can be of immense help.

For additional support and further integration of Practice Three, I strongly encourage you to listen to the guided meditations at www.AwarenessThatHeals.org.

PRACTICE FOUR

Inquiring from the Heart

*Inquiry gives us an immediate chance to shift from our
painful or fearful thoughts and feelings, to
seeking our greatest realistic potential.*

When you find yourself in a situation where you need guidance
and can only rely upon yourself, what are your options? From my
experience, one of the best approaches is asking yourself questions. But let
me immediately add: *not* just any kind of question.

Although most of us already ask ourselves questions about how we
might make positive changes in our lives, those questions are often asked
in ways that do not support us and do not bring healing. They can be
expressed with a negative edge like, "Why aren't you making more progress?" or "Why are you stuck in this feeling?" or "Can't you do something
better than get angry in this way?" Although this way of talking to ourselves takes the form of questions, these are expressed in accusatory tones
and are actually thinly veiled judgments which reinforce discouragement,
helplessness, and self-rejection.

I am proposing another way of questioning ourselves—one that works
for us rather than *against* us. I am proposing inquiry from the heart—from

a place that is informed by friendly mind, that rests in awareness of our challenges, and that moves us toward self-acceptance and greater freedom. The power of inquiring from the heart, when preceded by awareness and intention to heal, will help us to avoid fixating on our inner struggle. *We can pivot toward a positive direction.*

To help make this distinction clear, I've provided a few examples. The first shows what inquiring from the heart is *not*, and the others show what it *is*.

A client came to me asking the question, "I can't find a way to have a good love relationship. What's wrong with me?" I pointed out that her question didn't stimulate any curiosity, caring or alertness that could lead to any benefit. It became clear as we explored this together that she had tricked herself into believing she was coming from real curiosity. As we looked more closely, she was able to see that her question was quite self-critical as well as hurtful and discouraging. It sabotaged her efforts instead of supporting her to focus on small, practical steps she could take that could lead to the insights she needed. Seeing this led to a host of new questions that were aimed straight at her potential to respond more supportively to herself on a week-by-week basis. Ultimately, the question she asked was, "What can I do or how can I be different to increase my chances of finding a good love relationship?"

Here are the examples of the kinds of questions that are from the heart:

- How can I take the next realistic step to best care for myself?
- What is that one important thing that I want to do more often every day to feel more fulfilled? And: What would I have to give up to make space in my life to do that?
- What are the actual thoughts or actions that will best support me when I feel a challenging feeling such as anxiety, anger or sadness?

Questions such as these help you access your wisdom and intuitive intelligence while keeping your heart engaged; they help you contemplate and take actions that support your well-being; they help you respond effectively to a challenging situation or feeling. I've chosen the term *Inquiry* for this more specific, heartfelt and healing way of questioning yourself.

Inquiry is a practice that is sometimes part of the landscape of the world of spirituality. In this book, as these examples illustrate, I am not using the word to explore the more esoteric questions about our nature; rather, I'm using it to help us deepen our capacities to live a life closer to our most essential qualities and the beneficial parts of our character. Inquiry is an eminently practical tool to support our own well-being and, if we go far enough with it, we can use it to serve our greater world too.

Let me underscore that while inquiry is a practice in and of itself, it is also a vital part of the other seven practices in this book. Metaphorically speaking, inquiry and friendly mind are to all of the other practices what an "assist" is in basketball. *They are the practices that make the others more accessible and beneficial.* As you move through the book, you will see that both of them support your focus while you're in the middle of any of the other practices.

Inquiry from the heart is essential because, if we make this practice part of our lives, it is one of the key ways to focus our awareness in the direction of our own healing and fulfillment. It can also alert us when we are not heading in a healing direction. When we develop awareness that heals, an inquiry almost always arises to reveal a path to make things as good as they can be. Similarly, our friendly mind often provokes inquiries that help us address how we can *be with and tolerate* situations when no solution is presenting itself.

A friend of mine used to ask me in a discouraged and self-critical tone, "What's wrong with me? Why can't I find some upside income?" I was immediately struck by his question, because it was clearly not inquiry from the heart. It was inquiry from a place of profound self-rejection. It was essentially a way of berating himself, especially since he followed it with "What's my problem that I can't find a way to earn more money like most of my friends?" With time and greater self-caring, he almost totally gave up this kind of questioning—he could even do it with a smile—as he saw his self-criticism more clearly. He was able to see that he needed to change the nature and tone of the questions that he asked himself if he was going to feel better. He shifted the question so it could make a real difference, by asking, "Is there anything I can do this week that would be beneficial to support my livelihood?"

We often start out with vague questions that sabotage our contemplation by asking about a future that we can't really do anything about in the present. We may ask, "Why can't I ever lose this weight?" or "Why is it that I haven't found a greater sense of purpose in my life?" These questions can't really be answered because they are too futuristic and general. Also, curiously enough, they often keep us frustrated and stuck in the very problem we want to solve. Our questions always need to give us a real chance to respond or learn something new that could be beneficial.

Inquiry gives us an immediate chance to shift from our painful or fearful thoughts and feelings, to seeking our greatest realistic potential. It is an invitation for you to contemplate your life, inquire and give yourself a legitimate chance to respond. This allows you to move toward healing and the resolution of whatever challenge life has presented. Here is a short case study illustrating this practice of inquiry.

Cory

Cory woke up feeling agitated. He wasn't aware that he was so uptight until he heard himself say to his partner in a hostile tone, "Lexi, you woke me up again last night. How many times do I have to tell you to be more careful not to wake me up? You know I have a sleeping problem!" Later in the day Cory felt terrible, and asked himself the question, "Why do I feel so crappy and guilty?" He realized pretty quickly that he had been unfair and hostile with Lexi earlier that morning in the accusatory tone he used. He knew that she hadn't done it on purpose and that his mood had gotten the best of him. He asked himself, "What can I do to make amends and feel better?" The answer was obvious and he called her and gave a heartfelt apology for his negativity. He felt unburdened and relieved as he took full responsibility; it was clear that Lexi felt better too. He had found a sincere inquiry that produced a healing insight and action.

It is virtually inevitable that there will be a stage when we can't reliably find the clarity, compassion or the strength we seek and need. At these times it's natural to experience discouragement, doubt or just a desire to escape and avoid it all. Inquiry is an important tool to support us when we feel stuck in our challenging emotions and thoughts.

Inquiry can be effective whenever you're reactive, emotional, lost in thoughts or suffering in any way. For example, if you are upset with another for the way they reacted, you could ask, "How can I best re-approach the other person in both tone and words, and not lash out at them?" If you are feeling hurt or slighted by someone you love, you could ask yourself, "How can I ask for more caring in a way that sounds more like a request than a criticism?" There are also inquiries you can aim directly at yourself, such as "How can I be kinder toward myself when I am down on myself?" or "What attitudes do I need to change to guide me beyond self-judgment?" As I have mentioned before, it is not our feelings that are the problem—it is the way we respond (or don't respond) to them that is the key.

Inquiry will arise most naturally and meaningfully if we first are aware of any challenge we are feeling and then engage an intention to heal that will motivate us to ask the types of questions just mentioned above. Here are some examples:

- When you feel afraid and you remember to look inside for healing and peace, it often will lead to an inquiry, such as "How can I care for myself while I'm frightened?" or "How can I access more of my capacity for courage and safety?"

- As you're feeling angry and pause to feel your wish to be harmless, it is natural to ask, "How can I respond in a way to support being at greater peace with myself and the other person I'm dealing with?"

- When you're sad and remember you want to care for yourself, inquiry will most easily arise with "Is now a time to be gentle with myself and accept that this deep sadness is understandable, or is it a time to take an action that could help me along the way to feeling happier and more content?"

Practicing Inquiry from the Heart

Inquiry can go on intermittently for days in the background of your mind and heart when you are really interested in exploring a specific part of your life. When this happens, you want to be sure that you keep the same positive focus of questioning where it is clear that you are looking to support yourself.

Let me repeat: it is not only the *content* of the question that matters, but also the *way* you ask it. Most of us are more used to addressing ourselves with questions about why we behaved in a certain way, and we usually do this using an accusatory tone. Here we'll explore how you can practice inquiry in a way that is designed to create benefit without sabotaging yourself.

If you find your inquiries aren't keeping you on track or they seem negative, it could be because of the inner tone you are using to ask the question. Often it's difficult to hear or feel the tone of your questions, and you may find it very helpful to ask them out loud. When you do this, your tone becomes more apparent and obvious. In Practice Six, "Tuning into Tone of Voice," I will discuss this further. For now, let me say that the tone of your question to yourself is enormously consequential—it will reveal your self-love and self-care or, for that matter, self-rejection or withdrawal.

As mentioned, inquiry can also be practiced with a friend or partner. Here's how to go about it in more detail than what we've seen so far.

- First, a question is agreed upon. You explore the question as you seek the truth and guidance inside yourself.
- Set a time limit: 5-20 uninterrupted minutes.
- The person who is listening does so with receptivity, neutrality and attentiveness. They support you by making their best efforts not to react verbally or non-verbally to what you are sharing. This allows you to share what's happening without distraction, judgment or validation.
- If agreed upon ahead of time, the listener will repeat the question during the time period when they intuitively feel it's helpful. You do your best to focus on the question and give

sincere responses from your heart. You can also decide ahead
of time if the listener will give feedback at the end or not.

Once we're aware of disturbance or discomfort, inquiry is a simple
and profound tool available to us at any time and any place. Whether
your challenges are physical, psychological, relational or spiritual, you
can use this practice to seek deeper awareness and guidance from within.
It supports you to explore your feelings and needs as you address your
challenge. Inquiry can guide you toward your innate qualities of aliveness,
inspiration and curiosity. It can help you access the rich texture of your
inner world, enabling you to have a path to engage whenever you need
courage or strength, passion or tenderness.

Reflection Point: What question that you ask most frequently
takes you in a direction that causes hurt, fear or self-rejection?

Taking It Deeper: How do you want to reframe the question so
that it's the most beneficial to you?

Choosing a Question

The best questions are not random or abstract. The best questions are con-
nected to our present experience and near future.

While I have highlighted that your inquiry can be focused on something that is happening for you currently, you can also inquire about

something coming up in the near future. Here are three different time-related ways that you can use inquiry. With these examples, you can get a feel for how inquiry can work in these contexts and in various parts of your life.

Inquiry in the Moment

"What do I feel right now in my heart and body? What way do I need to think, act or be quietly introspective to best take care of my present experience? What are the body sensations, the needs, emotions or thoughts that are giving me clues to the question I need to ask right now?"

Example of Inquiry in the Moment

- If you experience fear or grief, you might inquire, "Can I see a likely source of these feelings based on recent situations, or is it perhaps something more to do with my past?" You could follow that up using the insights you get to make it more specific, and ask, "How can I care for these difficult feelings inside me, and are there any actions or thoughts that would be helpful for me to become focused on to find the best way to soothe these feelings?"

Inquiry of the Day

"What is the most essential way for me to be content and at peace through focus and sensitivity today? What are the thoughts, qualities or actions that I really want to encourage?"

Example of Inquiry of the Day

- You might become aware that you need to deal with personal relationship issues today. You might ask, "Of the people I know I am going to see today, which quality do I want to focus on that is most likely to change the value of my experience with each of them?"

Inquiry for the Near Future

"What are the most essential priorities to take care of this week? What do I need to let go of to create the space to make efficiency, fulfillment or peace most accessible? Where do I have the least trust that I will take good care of myself, and what do I need to focus on now in order to create the best opportunities for me in the near future?"

Example of Inquiry of the Near Future

- You may recognize that you need to prioritize time to improve physical fitness or health. A helpful question might be, "What days and times specifically am I ready to commit to working out weekly?" In order to give this a better chance to succeed, you could ask, "What is a way I am spending my time that I am ready to let go of so I will be able to follow one of my own suggestions?"

As insights emerge as a result of practicing inquiry, you may find that you want to gradually integrate changes into your life. The key is a sustained dedication to asking the most important and realistic questions that can serve you, and then responding to the guidance that resonates as true. *Real inquiry creates this extraordinary pivot from negative circular thinking and feeling to questions that lead to greater guidance, follow-through and well-being.*

As I have highlighted before, inquiry is most powerful when there is a strong charge around a situation: then, you'll be naturally engaged with it. If you don't significantly care about the issue, or if it isn't current for you, it will feel lukewarm, irrelevant and dull, and nothing beneficial is likely to happen. If this is the case, you can ask, "How can I feel more engaged or relaxed? I know I have to start where I am, with whatever I'm feeling or with whatever is important to me." Our state of mind or heart, when it is unsettled, is often a good indicator of questions that need to be asked. Inquiry doesn't mean you have to be excited or enthusiastic: there will be situations that will make that quite unlikely. Being authentic and true to where you are in that moment and inquiring from there, as a starting point, is what is needed.

Even if you are clear about what you are asking for, there are some questions that are too vague to be of support to you. For example, instead of asking, "What's the central purpose of my life?" which is unlikely to lead to any immediate and practical benefit, ask, "Where can I connect more deeply with something that is most likely to lead me to genuine satisfaction in the next day or two?" This second question is much more promising. It is current and relevant, and it has the potential to lead you to an increased understanding or ability to influence yourself. You will know you are on the right track when the question gives you a hint of feeling more alive, inspired or curious.

It is important to realize that the deeper your inquiry takes you, the more challenges you will discover. Looking at these discoveries as good news is so important here. Understanding this will allow you to both refocus if you do get lost in discouragement and to recognize it is a price worth paying in the pursuit of a more purposeful life.

An added benefit to the practice, which often brings clarity, peace and relief to my clients and me, is that these questions usually stop you from focusing on your negative thinking. Instead, you start pinpointing what realistic question will provide the most benefit to you in the present or in the near future.

Exercise: Ask yourself one question that matters to you. It may revolve around an unresolved issue that leaves you wanting to expand a particular quality in your heart.

Take 30 seconds to pause and then choose one of the following questions that most relates to you now:

- What is the most essential quality I need to develop to be true to myself and at peace with my life?
- What is my biggest blind spot where I cause pain to myself and others? What quality is most needed to lessen this pain?
- What unresolved situations or issues with other people do I have that need to be contemplated to support greater resolution and completion?

When we remain on the surface of things, it can seem that we have fewer challenges. Yet when we allow ourselves to go deeper, there is a better chance to see where we're blocked and create an opportunity to deal with it. Each time we feel a challenging emotion, inquiry can become a key part of our strategy.

Addressing Life's Challenges

As previously highlighted, it is always important to remember that when using inquiry you need to stay with it, even if it means asking the same question again and again over an extended period of time.

It is tremendously effective when we stay with our healing line of questioning and not switch back to thoughts or questions that are sabotaging or critical.

The process goes like this:

Awareness That Heals ⇒ Inquiry

Your question may be seeking a greater understanding of what you are experiencing and feeling in the moment or how to take a specific action. This can apply to both personal and professional challenges.

Personal

If you feel lousy, but don't know why, you can ask, "What is it that I feel, and what qualities and actions can I focus on to best take care of myself?" You are asking yourself how to take care of your feelings *while* exploring any actions that are necessary to take care of at the same time.

Professional

If you are unsure how to make a shift in your career, for example, you can ask with as much respect as possible, "What could my next move be?" If you don't know, then you recognize that this is the starting point of the inquiry, not the ending. This is the type of question that most likely needs to be repeated many times, with focus and without regressing into critical reactions or questions. You will need to explore whether your attention needs to be more on acceptance or gathering courage to make a move to a new situation. You will want to make sure that it really serves you and isn't just reactive.

If you find it difficult to identify a challenge, this is an indication that you're not yet making contact with a deeper level in yourself. Perhaps you've unconsciously believed that going deeper would affirm that there's something seriously wrong with you. I would ask you: After all, when we think about it, do we know anyone who doesn't have important challenges? So, if questions haven't been a significant part of your life, you might begin by asking, "Do I think the reason that I might not have questions is because I am afraid to address a particular conflict, or a scary or confusing part of my life?" You are likely to come to the realization that you need to see areas in your life that you may have ignored because you didn't feel enough hope, trust or courage to engage them. Inquiry will give you a chance to bring new awareness, intelligence and curiosity to this area.

Inquiries are most beneficial when they are imbued with qualities such as perseverance, presence and honesty. Inquiry isn't helpful or effective when it comes from a place of impatience, emotional cloudiness, looking for what's wrong or only asking from your head.

When judgments arise while in the midst of inquiring, gently return to your question the moment you are aware that you have wandered away from its intention. Remind yourself that inquiring never tries to force you to change anything. Instead, you are using present feelings and body sensations as clues to give the maximum information to effectively stay centered on asking your question and sensibly and supportively responding to it.

Working with Confusion

It is normal for my clients (and for that matter all of us) to have some confusion about how they can best take care of themselves. If that were not true, after all, there would be no reason for them to come to counseling in the first place. Over the years, I have learned to expect them to start out with some confusion. When they can acknowledge confusion, it is a sign of growing trust and courage to face the unknown.

The following situations, generated from my own life and those of my clients, illustrate how confusion can be transformed into well-being:

- You are confused about how much time you want to spend with a friend who is hurt because you haven't wanted to spend the same amount of time with them that they want with you. You can ask yourself, "How much time do I genuinely want to spend with this person? What amount of time do I think will give us the best chance of staying on a positive track with each other?" (As you can see—and I can't emphasize this enough—there are no shoulds here: you are just looking for the optimal fulfillment and close-ness.) As you try to sort this out and find the right balance, you ask yourself whether you are the type of person who gives yourself away too freely or if you tend to be too restrictive. As this question brings clarity, you look more carefully at the way and the amount of time —no matter how little it is—you want to spend with your friend in a respectful, caring way.

- You are confused about how to support yourself so that you can make the most out of an unusual free day where you have no demands. You may ask, "What is the number one thing I'd like to do tomorrow? How could I feel some new possible enjoyment, inspiration or intimacy?" Or you may ask, "If I can't figure out what to do with parts of my day, what attitude, specifically, will be most supportive while I'm in this confusion?"

- You are confused about why you have a habit of procrastinating about important things you know are good for you and will create relief or peace. So you ask yourself, "What is stopping me from taking the action I need?" When you don't receive a response that leads to an insight you might say, "Even though I can't see what's needed yet, I can hear my friendly mind reminding me that this is difficult to see: it's encouraging perseverance."

Part of the evolution of inquiry is letting go of the expectation for instant gratification. It supports you to develop focus, discipline and contemplativeness.

▼

Reflection Point: Here are some common areas of confusion: financial issues, relational areas, family impasses, friendship conflicts, lifestyle decisions, health issues and difficult emotions. Can you call to mind a moment you were confused about something in one of these areas and that you think you will probably repeat? See what question you could have asked yourself to give yourself the best chance for support and clarity.

Taking It Deeper: Now, staying with that same question, give yourself some time to explore it more deeply. Notice if you can find a place that is supportive of yourself.

Exploring Meditation and Prayer

Inquiry may naturally lead us to meditation or prayer, which are practices that are included in various traditions from around the world. I see them as tools that lead us to support ourselves more effectively when we're aware of a challenge and have engaged a healing intention.

For example, if you ask yourself, "How can I best take care of myself?" your inner guidance might encourage meditation or prayer. And it is also true that meditation and prayer can create the motivation to go back into inquiry!

As I've mentioned already, all the practices in this book intertwine and are interconnected. And, as you can see, there are no rules as to where an intention to heal or an inquiry might lead you. So, meditation and prayer are two other dynamic practices that you have at your disposal and can use freely whenever they are called for.

Here is a closer look at each of these powerful ways that are connected with inquiring from the heart.

Meditation

When we are facing a difficulty, awareness that heals and inquiry may lead us to meditation. It's often because we need to go within and to be free from the interference of our mind's incessant activity.

By "meditation" I am not referring only to sitting for an extended period of time while we keep our minds still. Many experienced meditators and teachers recognize that this can be a very limited view. (This is a significant reason why many people believe that they can't meditate. This fixed idea prevents many from even starting to practice.)

I believe that a more helpful way of presenting what is done in meditation, especially at the start, is: *being present or mindful for moments at a time*. Even the most skeptical realize that, in their own way, they have experienced elements of meditation already. And, this is something that even the most driven, busy and distracted people do on occasion without even trying. Whenever you notice what's happening in the moment, you are glimpsing the beginnings of meditation. These moments can happen when we, for example, look a baby in the eyes, feel the wind blow, watch the sun set, nurture a pet, make love, laugh or counsel. These kinds of moments mark one of the beginning experiences of meditation; another word for it at the beginning and intermediate stages is what is commonly understood as presence.

Most of us at the beginning—or even after years of practice—have experienced moments when we have felt like a "failure." We've been

conditioned in our society to accept as normal a never-ending and uninterrupted stream of thoughts and feelings. Because of this, it commonly
takes an extended time to train our minds. It's like becoming an athlete,
a musician or an artist—it requires practice. Tsoknyi Rinpoche, one of
the premier meditation teachers in the West, says that ten seconds of real
silence is quite an accomplishment. Knowing this, we can then allow ourselves to meditate without reaching for perfection or thinking we are not
doing it right. For both beginners and advanced meditators, it is profound
to value the subtlety of real presence no matter how long it lasts.

The following is an exercise that has been beneficial to me, my clients
and my friends, regardless of our familiarity with meditation.

Exercise: Let yourself have a simple goal, such as staying present
for a few moments. Settle your body in its most comfortable
position and stay as relaxed and present as possible. You can
listen to your breath going in and out, listen to sounds, or feel
body sensations. Spend 3 to 5 minutes meditating, and allow the
priority to be a few seconds of presence.

Many friends, clients and colleagues have benefited from using a version of this breathing practice with awareness as a beautiful way to go to
sleep. You can either give yourself a head start with a relaxed meditation
and greater peace for the body or drop into a restful sleep: a win-win.

Prayer
Prayer, as I am using it, is a pure yearning or even a form of longing for
one or more elements of compassion to manifest. Prayer supports us to
expand the urge to open our hearts to more of life. We aren't necessarily

praying to God (although it doesn't exclude praying to God). What we are praying for is a particular quality such as courage, compassion or empathy.

For example:

- May I be as compassionate as possible.
- May I be guided to my natural strength so I can set boundaries in a graceful way.
- May my tone of voice nourish and be healing to those around me.
- May I be as present as possible in this moment.

Prayer can be practiced at any time or in any place. It can also be formal or informal. Many spiritual teachings, especially in the Buddhist traditions, use "purifying intention" as their form of prayer; it is similar to the more Judeo-Christian and Muslim practice of praying to God, except you can be praying to reach your true nature, not an externalized God. Some people pray to nature or existence itself. Some believe there is no God and find their personal way to address their suffering or hopes in life—and they still pray to what might be felt as the purest part of their own heart that they are longing to reach.

Other examples:

- When times are most difficult, may I be able to ask, both inside myself and outside as needed, for a gentler heart.
- May I remember to ask for help, especially when I feel most lost.
- May my asking to access greater humility allow me to let go of my entitlements and demands.
- May I find as much courage as possible when I'm frightened and at the same time be kind and accepting of my fears.
- May I bring empathy and goodwill to as many people as possible.

It is also worth noting that some of the prayers above might seem similar to affirmations. As I described in the first chapter, the difference is that when you affirm something, you do so as though you believe it has already happened or you want it to be true. An example of an affirmation is "I am a loving person." With prayer, you are sincerely asking for something you need from outside of yourself or from inside yourself. An example is, "May I be supported to find as much love as possible." Here, you are not attempting to believe in something; instead, you are attempting to access the quality itself with your intention. You know you don't have it yet and you are reaching for it. You don't expect to believe in it, but rather are developing your capacity to experience and convey it.

Prayer and inquiry can be combined with our yearnings in other ways. You can play with "what-is-obvious" by asking questions that sound absurd to the conscious mind, such as "Would I rather be afraid or feel more courage?" Or "Would I rather be blindly competitive or do my best with respect for others?" Or "Would I rather be patient or impatient with my child?" Even though the answers are obvious, the key is that by asking these questions consciously, you sharpen and deepen your motivation and desire for greater kindness and compassion, both for yourself and others.

I have seen many of my clients' lives graced by using prayer. It has catalyzed so many quality moments of peace and ease. Prayer is such a helpful practice when we are feeling what we don't want to or can't feel what we do want to. A little prayer can make a huge difference at these times, because instead of struggling with a feeling or lack of one, we can shift our focus, or place ourselves on a path to find our sincerest intention.

Guiding Our Lives

It is both reassuring and inspiring to start to get the knack of using your mind and heart in a way that is designed to benefit you and those around you. And it can be easy to slip back into ordinary habits of questioning yourself in hurtful ways. So it is like any kind of learning—it takes practice, sincerity and discipline. Even though it seems like common sense to be interested in asking how you can be more fulfilled or how you can heal where it is most needed, this is not how most of us respond in our lives. It is important to realize this gap between conditioned and unfulfilling habits and our potential. You will need to remind yourself over and over to break the imprinting of past patterns.

Key Messages

With questioning and inner seeking, we learn to witness, and trust in, our innate hunger to find our own compassion or wisdom. We are led to insights and understandings in a whole new way. As we develop inquiry, we move from intellectual curiosity to something akin to a love affair with discovering the truth about life and ourselves. We naturally discriminate between questions that are veiled judgments and ones that are designed to serve our lives and be of greatest benefit to others as well.

Through time, we develop a deeper trust that the questions we are focusing on are heartfelt ones from our wisest intelligence—questions that are most likely to move us toward healing and well-being. Here we can find that we no longer spin in confusion or continuous destructive thoughts for long. Instead, our practice can truly evolve to a point where we're drawn to feel curious, which leads us to trust our inquiries and allow responses to our questions to arise with an ease that isn't forced or pressured. In the answers and guidance to our sincere inquiries, we find that our own best counsel and wisest mentor are often inside ourselves.

The pressure that we might have felt in the earlier stages of practicing inquiry is reduced or gone *because* we are invested just as much in the process of asking as we are in finding the guidance or answer that may come. We can feel the solid confidence that the truth of our question will reveal itself: we know that forcing answers will not help. We are learning to steadily open and be available, interested and patient. We are treating ourselves as a friend because this kind of inquiry is another way of saying, "How can I help and care for you?"

Eventually inquiry can become first nature. By "first nature," I mean that whenever an issue or emotional challenge is happening, a question oriented toward healing effortlessly appears. In fact, at a certain point in your practice, it doesn't need the provocation of a difficult situation to be activated. Because of the prior experience and benefits, the healing intention and inquiry are so well-established that you almost automatically become the questioner.

A routine way of thinking about it at this stage might be, "Why would I do anything else?" There is a gratitude that comes with the self–compassionate trust you have. As continuity becomes first nature, if the question evolves or changes, it becomes a more precise upgrade of the original question so that it allows you to receive even more benefit from it. For example, you might start with asking, "What is needed for me to feel closer to my lover?" As a part of your contemplation, it might become clear that the main issue that will support your love has to do with trust. You could then upgrade the question to "What is needed for us to cultivate a deeper trust or express more affection?"

Inquiry, when used in this way, becomes the practice that guides you toward the direction that will be most healing—it will expand your sense of well-being. The insights and realizations will naturally come from your inquiries. And the gratitude for having a simple method to access what you most need becomes expansive.

Integrating the Chapter: Inquiries

1. What are the questions that you still ask yourself that are really veiled statements of criticism? (For example, "What's wrong with me?" "Can't I do better than that after all my years of working on myself?")

2. What specific questions do you need to ask yourself that will serve your life and replace the old questions that haven't worked for you?

3. What is the most challenging emotional state where you're most likely to forget to use inquiry to support yourself? What would be the best reminder, and what question would be most healing to ask while you're in that state?

4. What is the inquiry that is most needed to inspire you to develop a compassionate quality that you usually avoid?

For additional support and further integration of Practice Four, I strongly encourage you to listen to the guided meditations at www.AwarenessThatHeals.org.

Developing Wisdom Guidance

*The best way to access wisdom guidance is to combine
awareness of a present or anticipated challenge, accessing
an intention to heal and inquiring about what is needed.*

Where can we find our most valuable guidance in life?
As our exploration of inquiry reveals, the most valuable wisdom
in life can be found deep within us—and we are often unaware of this
great potential source of guidance. This is totally understandable: after all,
few of us have been taught how to look inside ourselves.

We never learned how to question or to receive guidance from ourselves and, consequently, haven't been shown how to access it. Thus, our
most potent wisdom most often remains largely untapped.

I call this our *wisdom guidance*. It is *a way of supporting ourselves that
leads us first to our thoughts and then to the actions and qualities that will
guide us toward healing and well-being.* With practice and experience, we
can learn how to both connect with and benefit from our wisdom guidance, which awaits our sincerest heartfelt requests.

Many of the practices we explore in this book are intended to support
your access to, and sensitivities and capacities for, kindness, generosity

and self-caring. Wisdom guidance is another key practice and reveals itself as simple guiding thoughts that will likely suggest a course of action or developing specific qualities in whatever emotion or situation you find yourself in.

In the first four chapters, we explored awareness that heals, friendly mind, moving from self-rejection toward self-compassion and inquiry. All of them, especially inquiry, can help us access our wisdom guidance and persevere when access is difficult. To define it from a different perspective, our wisdom guidance *frames in word and tone the message that is most supportive to our present life experience*. It's a blend of timely intuition and intelligence that leads us to greater peace or fulfillment.

Wisdom guidance is *not* that voice inside our head that misdirects us, or judges and moralizes about how we should behave or act, and it's essential that we be able to distinguish between the two. In this chapter, we'll be exploring how to find the voice of your wisdom guidance, how to distinguish it from your conditioned, moralistic judgments and other self-rejecting inner talk and how to activate it so that it can become a source of guiding direction for you and others.

The best way to access wisdom guidance is to combine awareness of a present or anticipated challenge, accessing an intention to heal and inquiring about what is needed. When you become aware of the specific challenge that you need to work with, you can ask the question that could most help you in the situation you're in. When you are feeling agitated with someone, you might ask, "What can I say to that person and how can I say it so that it will most likely support our well-being?" And: "What can I say to myself and how can I say it so that it will support kindness toward myself while I'm feeling this tightness inside?"

At the beginning, some of my clients have found it helpful to write down the wisdom guidance that arises in response to their inquiries and stay focused on integrating these messages. This helps you keep the questions and responses specific and have the benefit of seeing a record of your own guidance as it evolves. It is important that you don't force or pressure yourself to find answers. *This is by far the biggest danger point for losing faith in wisdom guidance.*

We don't realize that in many situations we are trying to change generations of conditioning and habits. We need a lot of patience, self-compassion and courage to work with this stage of our evolution. It is helpful to call on friendly mind when we can't reach the guidance we need. It will invariably remind us with a statement like, "Good for you that you are trying to find what will bring deeper fulfillment. Of course, it may take a while, and when you are sincere and haven't received any guidance yet, well, this is the time to be most trusting and supportive of yourself (even when you can't feel it)."

Maitlin

Maitlin—a former client of mine—had a mammogram and was told that she had a spot in her breast that looked suspicious. Her mother had breast cancer, and her worst fear was that the same would happen to her. She was preparing herself for further testing. She was panicked that she had to immediately find the answer so she could feel safer. I supported her to find a question that wouldn't create this pressure so that she could have the best chance to access her wisdom guidance. With a sigh of relief, she asked herself, "How can I best take care of myself while I am waiting for two weeks to get my next test results?" She started by finding words and a tone that supported her to be accepting of her anxiety. Her wisdom guidance said, "Of course you're nervous—that's natural—you care about your health and quality of life. Be kind toward your feelings. Stay present and keep developing resiliency and courage."

This expression of wisdom guidance allowed her to be much softer and more realistic with herself. She recognized how natural it was to be afraid and anxious. But she appreciated how hard she'd worked on herself and knew she was in the best place to be caring and resourceful no matter what happened.

Here are two examples of what it means to develop wisdom guidance in everyday life:

- Doug was feeling helpless as he watched his brother's addiction. He'd tried everything he could for the past few years and no longer felt he had good options to intervene. He was uncomfortable with any thought of giving up on someone he loved, so he inquired, "Can I find a way to be okay until I see another viable and realistic way to help?" His wisdom guidance supported him by saying, "I trust your most wholesome love and your best efforts. You've done everything you can see to do: you can't control the outcome." Doug accepted that he might always feel some pain in relationship to his brother, and that it was a part of the price he was paying for the depth of his love. This insight was a source of great relief to him.
- Joan's father passed away after a sudden illness. She didn't get a chance to say goodbye or resolve some unspoken feelings and express her love. Joan was so caught in her sadness that it was almost disabling. After we worked on this a while together, she asked herself, "What thoughts would help me most care for my sadness?" She heard, "It's perfectly natural that you feel sad. Appreciate your love for him, and your innocence: life's circumstances didn't allow

you to have a chance to say goodbye. Your love is obvious; please send it to him." Inside herself and then out loud, she said from her heart to her father, "I love you and wish I could have protected you. I'm so sorry and I'm so grateful to you for all the love and tenderness you gave to me." This allowed her to not be bottled up and to accept more deeply her love and loss.

Reflection Point: Think of a current situation that is challenging and where you could be supported with an inquiry and wisdom guidance such as you've seen in the examples above.

Taking It Deeper: What words of guidance come to you as you think of this situation? Allow yourself the time you need to find them.

Starting with Awareness

As explored in Practice One, we need to be *aware* of our challenges before we can take our first steps to guide ourselves toward our wisdom and compassion. Many of us believe we are "fine" when under the surface we are actually not. Often we have a fleeting awareness that something inside us doesn't feel right, but it remains at that level of awareness.

Allowing ourselves to feel and take notice of our internal pain is not a familiar or automatic process for most of us. To foster our capacity to do this, we need to be as gentle as possible with where we are when we take a look inside and ask ourselves, "How am I *really* doing?" Being gentle with ourselves as we ask this question gives us the best chance to open our hearts and minds. The first step in wisdom guidance, as in all the other practices in this book, is to deepen our awareness of our more challenging feeling states so that we don't just operate from our knee-jerk reactions to them. (You may find it helpful to listen to the guided meditation that is designed to deepen this capacity for loving curiosity called "How Are You Doing?" It is available on the website www.AwarenessThatHeals.org.)

When you become familiar with your challenges, you can develop a shorthand where you use just a few words that will steer you in the direction of activating your heart, your intelligence and the qualities and actions most needed in the situation. You may say, "Relax, stay receptive or be sensitively honest." But no matter what your guidance is, it is attempting to lead you to a more fulfilling quality of life, and greater peace.

Through the sincerity and depth of your practice of both inquiry and wisdom guidance, you will have greater access to that compassionate and essential voice inside that represents your best response to whatever is needed in the moment and situation. When you look at your past, you may find you're already familiar with these kinds of sensitive responses. You very likely used different words than "wisdom guidance" to describe them. For example, you have used this wisdom in the moments you've been able to pause and think better of striking out in anger. And perhaps, in these instances, your wisdom guidance, or whatever you've called it, revealed the frustrated underlying need that caused you to be mad or made you aware of the damage it would do if expressed.

You'll also have applied your wisdom when you listened to and acted upon thoughts suggesting you be more caring toward another person rather than choosing to withdraw or punish them. When your thoughts guide you to be gentle and sensible with yourself or a friend instead of being unnecessarily critical, that is also your wisdom guidance leading you. It reveals itself when an important challenge is at hand that requires discipline, and you say to yourself, "It's time to concentrate." In this chapter, then, we're deepening access to your wisest thoughts by helping you to both identify them more easily and focus on connecting with them when you most need them.

The Origins of Wisdom Guidance

My own journey with wisdom guidance began around the age of eighteen, when I first remember yearning to have a life filled with more meaning. When I became a counselor at a summer camp in Big Bear, California, the camp director introduced me to a spiritual teaching. His approach emphasized the importance of dedicating ourselves to good intentions. While I eventually devoted myself to the training, I initially viewed this approach with an underlying attitude of skepticism.

I had good reason to be unsure. Until that time, I had not found a single person who described, let alone lived in accordance with, values, systems or religions that deeply touched my heart. My best, and only, compassionate role models were a couple of high school teachers and friends, but their impacts weren't powerful enough to support me to experience a more caring heart as a central priority. This isn't surprising given the extreme emphasis our culture places on success, power, endless youthfulness and recognition.

It was hard to tolerate feeling like a stranger in a strange land because those priorities seemed so secondary to love and honesty. In response to this, I developed a frustrated, critical way of speaking to others that had a sarcastic edge to it. At the time, I was actually proud of what I viewed as my "quick wit." It was only later that I could see this was my way of defending myself against my own pain and alienation.

After I had practiced this new teaching for about a year, however, I started to see that my emphasis on the negative and my pride in "cleverly" putting others down through humor, was bringing me down at the same time. When I realized how my critical attitude was causing suffering to others and myself, I sincerely asked, "How do I break a habit that has been here for so long?"

As my thought process progressed and I made this genuine inquiry for my wiser voice to speak to me, I received the response: "Remember the positive." I repeated this phrase to myself several times a day, even when I wasn't feeling negative. I practiced and planted seeds everywhere I could, as I anticipated daily opportunities to shift from one set of reactive motivations to cultivating another set with a positive intention. As time passed, this mantra would show up in my mind as many as one hundred times a day. More and more often, I'd catch myself in the middle of a sarcastic joke or an annoyed reaction, and the phrase "Remember the positive" would enter my mind. This helped remind me to keep the focus on my heart and was really a quantum shift away from how I'd lived since I entered college. (A note: This was very different from positive thinking, as the thoughts that were positive were inspiring me to make a change in how I actually responded.) It was the beginning of creating a solid foundation, which I could then trust to enable me to increase my inquiries and gain more and more access to my wisdom guidance. This process continues to this day.

At the beginning, I sometimes couldn't easily distinguish the difference between my genuine guidance and other thoughts. So I began paying more attention to the quality of my attitude, and that proved to be an important differentiator. When I looked inside for guidance while still being caught in anger or being demanding, I could see that these thoughts frequently led to a suggestion that kept me circling in negativity.

However, when I inquired in a sincere way and with an intention to heal, the response came back in a positive tone—and it included a message that would never intentionally create harm, and most often would create benefit. It was also quite evident that inquiring in a way that was looking for the very best caring possibility made a huge difference. For example, when I felt exhausted and asked in a weary tone, "How can I possibly take care of my energy, given how tired I am?" I would hear something like, "It's hard to imagine how there's anything more you can do, given how bad you feel." When I found a place inside that was a genuine wish, prayer or intention, like, "How can I best take care of my energy considering how tired I am?" I almost always would hear a suggestion that was beneficial, such as "I know it's hard and I think it's best to spend one hour focused on taking care of your business and then rest." It didn't always create instantaneous results, but I intuitively knew I was on the right track.

Wisdom Guidance Is Not Judgmental

Our wisdom guidance never seeks to judge us. It is always neutral and friendly, and it does not punish us. Instead, it is more like "a bearer of truth," supporting us to move toward what will bring the most peace, fulfillment and inspiration to us. Wisdom guidance doesn't take sides because it is dedicated to our own, and everyone else's, well-being.

This doesn't mean that our wisdom guidance is always going to be soft or gentle in its message. Frequently it can be a "firm teacher." It can be a call for strength when you need to jolt yourself awake. Sometimes if you have been asleep in a deep habit, you will need to have an intense voice to wake yourself up. Suzanne's story below highlights the non-judgmental quality of wisdom guidance.

Suzanne

Suzanne, a successful attorney, offered her services to a commercial law firm that did pro bono work for start-up inner city and international charities providing services to people in poverty around the world. I was brought in as a consultant to assist the board, and I could see the indignation etched on Suzanne's face when she was at a meeting with Arthur, the CEO of the non-profit team.

After the meeting I invited her to sit down and asked if she wanted help. "Yes, I'm so bottled up and exasperated," she began. "When I agreed to work with Arthur, I was promised a lot of help. I made an agreement at the time to take half of my usual salary, assuming I'd only be working part-time. But during the last year and a half, I've been working up to eighty hours a week because I never got the support I needed, despite asking repeatedly for the help that was promised. Now we're about to have a meeting to set the agenda for the coming years and I'm so freaked out and pissed off, I don't think I want to work with these people anymore. I don't know if this is my anger talking or not."

I asked her, "Is there any possibility you could feel your sincerity and your genuine love for this work and this vision?" I waited, and then asked. "Can you say what you just told me, but this time, can you try expressing it through what your heart really longs for?"

She then pretended to be sitting with Arthur, and told him exactly what she wanted with tenderness, strength and sincerity. She reiterated what she had told me with a sincere tone, "I really want to ask that you pay me the fair hourly amount that we agreed to for the number of hours that I am working." Then with a pause and a softer tone, she said, "I want to find the incredible goodwill and inspiration that we had at the beginning."

And at that point, we went into the meeting. Suzanne had all the best intentions at the beginning, but her frustration and agitation took over and she began to attack Arthur. She regressed to what she'd felt at the start of our process and wasn't able to access her intention to come from her heart. With severe agitation, she said, "Arthur, this is what I want," and followed this with the ways that she had been mistreated and how he should rectify them.

She clearly needed another rehearsal. We met again, and I suggested she return to keeping her focus on what it was she needed in detail and expressing it in a new respectful way. Suzanne started out being angry and gradually softened her tone. She found her capacity to express her sincere needs and thought about the next meeting with a newly felt sense of self-confidence and ease.

Suzanne set up another meeting with Arthur. They were able to reach an agreement about how to move forward in a way that felt fair to both of them. Suzanne told me later she knew that she still had work to do to stabilize her capacity to speak with a tone of sincerity instead of expressing her anger. She also knew she had made vital progress in her personal awareness.

Suzanne's decision to change that day, aided by her wisdom guidance, allowed for the delivery of a service in the third world that affected hundreds of thousands of people.

To know whether you are hearing your wisdom guidance and not an inner critical voice, you need to be aware of whether you notice any tightness or moralistic judgment. If you do, let it go as much as you can. When your wisdom guidance is responding to anger, its tone may well be passionate, persistent and strong, but it doesn't contain any punitive judgments. *It is always <u>for</u> something—never against.* This is a key distinction. You can be passionately for justice instead of putting your focus on being angry at injustice. You can be strong when you tell your lover what you'd like, rather than becoming frustrated or angry about what you don't like.

Our wisdom guidance is rooted in supporting us, while not compromising what is true. If you need to scream passionately at yourself, your wisdom guidance will let you know that you are screaming *for* yourself—not *against* yourself. You are not treating yourself as an object, but are rather united with yourself. You are telling yourself, "Let's wake up," rather than, "You should wake up." This intensity is the loving passion emanating from you and toward you. It creates more wholeness, helping you to remember the totality of yourself instead of feeling a separation or that you have done something wrong.

Imagine, for example, that you have just failed to get a promotion that you expected. You might use this inquiry: "How can I deal with these aggressive feelings I have toward myself and my boss because I have failed to get the promotion that I deserve?"

You might hear this guidance in response to your inquiry:

- Be as harmless as you can be.
- Ask yourself, "Do I need to communicate more, take some constructive action or come to a deeper inner acceptance of my anger?"
- Appreciate your focus on what will give you the best chance for peace and resolution, instead of stewing in anger.
- Access your sincerity and see if you are doing everything possible.

Reflection Point: Can you remember a poignant time when you looked inside yourself for guidance but then followed a moralistic or judgmental message that had been bred into you since childhood? What do you wish you had suggested to yourself or to another? Is the difference between these two pathways clearer to you now or do you need to explore it more?

Taking It Deeper: Can you remember an important time when you were able to turn inward and help a friend or yourself instead of staying uninvolved or being judgmental? Did you find that this allowed you to take care of a need? If so, this was an example of your wisdom guidance.

Wisdom Guidance and Your Tone

Tone of voice is so fundamental that the next chapter is devoted entirely to that. It is another healing practice in this book. Here, however, I want to highlight how beneficial it is when we pay close attention to our tone as we receive or ask for our guidance. It is as important, and often even more important, than the words themselves.

You might say to yourself, "I need to open my heart." This can have either a tone of "You dumb fool," or "Give it your very best effort with sincerity and kindness." It is vital that you be on the alert for the difference in your internal tone as you experience your inner contemplation. We want to learn to treat ourselves with as much empathy and compassion as possible.

It is our tone that conveys the benefits of empathy, tenderness, warmth—and even strength, if needed. *When the message and the tone are united in this way, it sets us up to receive the optimal elements of wisdom guidance.*

Wisdom Guidance Is Responsive to the Present

Wisdom guidance, as it is awakened, responds uniquely to each situation to support our well-being. It therefore becomes a flexible resource that will help you intelligently and sensitively address whatever is happening in your current life. Accessing it is always useful.

Your wisdom guidance serves to support the expansion and awakening of your heart, no matter how much you may be hurting or afraid. Asking questions, such as "How can I help myself when I feel like this?" or "How can I best support myself right now?" helps you to connect to your wisdom guidance.

Your wisdom guidance will make practical suggestions, such as:

- Stay harmless in both your tone and words.
- Rest until you feel more refreshed.
- This is difficult for you so take a moment to be as gentle with yourself as possible.

All of these, said in a time of contemplation, are ways wisdom guidance will propose for you to take care of the circumstance you are facing. Through time and practice, you will learn to trust this part of you. Hearing your guidance is like having an excellent counselor nearby to support yourself when you most need it.

Blind spots, negative triggers and emotional fixations often block our wisdom guidance. Negative thoughts, such as "I am not smart enough to get this," "I hate it when she does that to me," or "I'll never find the one

I love," can serve as red flags to help you spark a genuine intention to be more self-compassionate. This in turn will encourage you to move toward further inquiries.

One of the beauties of wisdom guidance (along with inquiry) is that you can do it anywhere—and anytime. You can do it standing still or on the move. You can do it while others are around or when you are on your own. You can do it at work, in the middle of a fight, when you first wake up, when you go to bed or when you are not feeling well and you don't know why. The dynamism of it and the fact that it is a tool that is available to you all the time means that it can quickly and easily become your wise inner support system: trustworthy, aware and caring no matter where you are.

Reflection Point: What is the most common feeling or situation that you find yourself in where you could use a simple guiding statement to most support yourself? What would you ask yourself so that you can be guided to your wisdom?

Taking It Deeper: Can you see a situation where a person close to you could be helped by having any specific guidance that comes to you? What would you say?

Examples of Practicing Wisdom Guidance

As you read the following examples, you'll see that each contains a beginning inquiry that catalyzes wisdom guidance as it is sincerely explored.

When you are aware that you are feeling alone

John's two closest friends moved out of town and he was a bit disoriented by how alone he felt. He developed a new habit where, each night after he came home, he just sat and watched TV—something he'd never done before in his life. He wrestled with his feelings and found himself repeating the same self-critical judgments, such as "What's wrong with you that you can't make new friends?"

He began his inquiry with:
"How can I feel more connected to myself and those around me?"

He heard this guidance:
- Be aware of your loneliness with as much kindness and patience as possible. Recognize it is likely to take some time to develop similar friendships.
- If you aren't sure what to do, keep asking yourself, "What new places can I explore, and who could I call that might lead me toward meeting potential new friends or becoming a new friend for somebody? What other possibilities are there?"
- In the interim, realize that, at times like this, learning how to value your aloneness is also a very worthy focus.

When you are aware of facing pain or illness

Joan, thirty-five, had been active throughout her entire life. She noticed she was sleeping more than usual and had a lot less energy during the day too. She attributed it to recent life stressors. When it persisted for a few months she went to the doctor and learned she very likely had chronic fatigue syndrome. Because a sure diagnosis is difficult and her symptoms persisted, she was struggling inside to push herself to resume her normal activities even though it was obvious she couldn't.

She began her inquiry with:
"What do I need to support my healing now?"

She heard this guidance:
- Be as gentle as possible with yourself and only do what is most important in order to conserve your energy.
- Rest when you need to, and recognize it as a form of self-love and care.
- Recognize that your situation would be very difficult for anyone, continue to adjust your expectations and be realistic.

When you become aware that you haven't been able to find love in your life

Jason had always dated and had a few one-year relationships since he'd graduated from college ten years earlier. He was getting to an age where his closest friends were getting married and having children. He started to have doubts about his ability to have a sustaining love relationship even though he didn't see any reason why he couldn't. Attending so many weddings was getting him down and he was left wondering what was wrong with him. He realized that he was working on himself and doing everything possible to create opportunities.

He began his inquiry with:

"Is there anything I can do or ways I can be to give myself a better chance to find the love I seek?"

Given that he was confident that he was making his best efforts including going to therapy to explore blind spots, he heard:

- Appreciate that you have made and are continuing to make your best efforts and see the absurdity of wanting to do more than your realistic very best. You can say with great surety: "My best efforts are good enough."

- Realize that you can't ever be at peace with yourself as long as you follow archaic conditioned standards that demand that you should be in a relationship and that you can't be a whole person without it.

- If you can't recognize the truth in these thoughts, then connect with someone who knows you have devoted yourself to being available to relationships, who can laugh with you for judging your best efforts and can guide you with support.

When you are facing fear

Kathy loved her work and was promoted to a position in administration where she was responsible for supervising other people. She loved this because her people skills were strong. However, with the position came the task of making presentations to higher-ups in her company. This meant showing her team's PowerPoint presentations and speaking to as many as fifty people, all of whom were executives at her company. She was paralyzed with fear to the point where the thought of speaking made her begin to feel physically ill. She managed the first few presentations—barely. Despite her accomplishment she was so miserable she was considering quitting her job.

She began her inquiry with:

"How can I face my fear more directly but not be overwhelmed or undermined by it?"

She heard this guidance:

- Fear, I'm gathering both the courage not to be dominated by you and the wisdom not to allow you to run my life or make my decisions.
- Realize that everyone feels fear when any new scary challenge appears. It's perfectly natural that you are afraid. Remember that anyone who lives life fully has to have moments of fear or there isn't growth. Trust yourself as you experience the fear.
- Stay focused. See that making your best efforts—*especially* when you can't feel the good results—is one of the most valuable expressions of your own wisdom.

Utilizing Your Wisdom Guidance in Relationships

As you learn to ask the questions that are most important to support your intimacy, you can then be guided to respond in ways that will help you continue to grow and expand your love. Reminding ourselves about our own patterns in relationships and about how we can grow by being more open with our partner and ourselves are two of the key ways that wisdom guidance can support us.

Julie

Julie had a heart that would not only nurture her own family, but also pretty much anyone she would meet. She had been married for twenty years and had been fairly contented—until recently. She had a fleeting awareness that she would like her husband, Michael, to be more considerate and attentive when she was upset or sick, but because this awareness was not stable, she could never express these deeper needs. During the past few years things had changed, and Michael had become more withdrawn and unmotivated. He attempted to drown this out by increasing the amount of alcohol he consumed. This brought them into therapy with me, and it became clear that she felt such "empathy" (or what could more accurately be called codependency) for him that she made continuous rationalizations for why he couldn't find his motivation or enthusiasm for anything.

Over the year that followed, Julie began to see how much of an enabler she was for Michael. She became aware of how she had suppressed her own needs for loving attention, appreciation and a true sharing of responsibility at many levels of life. She realized she wanted to stay aware of her needs. She was inclined to keep forgetting them, even though she would have many epiphanies about her patterns. When she learned how to use wisdom guidance, she heard, "Remember your needs and express them clearly," over and over again. Every time she heard her wisdom guidance, she smiled as she asked herself, "What do I need now?" She became devoted to increasing her awareness in this way. She realized and expressed her need for nurturing, attention and affection, and the need to be sensitively assertive in the areas that were affected in the relationship. She made it clear that these needs were not negotiable and this firmness got Michael's attention.

He went through various stages of avoidance, but gradually realized how valid her needs were. This was vastly transformational for their marriage. He saw, in his most honest moments, that he was self-centered, and that her prior denial had helped him to avoid himself. The result of addressing her own needs was not beneficial just to Julie—it helped wake Michael up as well.

As you use your awareness and develop your ability to practice inquiry more effectively, wisdom guidance will help you to stay focused on maximizing the best outcomes for any challenge that you're facing. You will also be encouraging the deepening of your sense of intuition, humor and heart.

Your wisdom guidance also fosters an inner caring and trust in yourself. You will discover, when your heart is aching or your feelings are raw and tender, that your wisdom guidance will help you realize you are deserving of empathy and kindness.

Wisdom Guidance Goes Beyond Our Feelings

Have you ever noticed how much we identify with our emotions? When we do this, we may find ourselves saying, "I don't feel like myself today," because we believe we are a certain kind of person. What we are really indicating when we say this is, "I am not experiencing my ordinary emotional state." We are so identified with our ordinary state that we believe something is wrong with us when we have feelings that are outside of our normal parameters. This is where a lot of our extra pain originates. If we find that we are feeling down, anxious or in pain in a way that isn't typical for us, we think we aren't ourselves. We then not only have to deal with the original feelings, but also with the underlying sense of failure that comes from feeling that we should be some other way. This type of self-rejection was explored earlier. In these situations, it is helpful to ask yourself, "Is it realistic for me to think I can change my feelings with a snap of my fingers?"

If we take a close look at how rarely we are able to change our feelings through an act of will, we will see that it is a futile endeavor to make this effort. Our wisdom guidance suggests, "Rather than attempting to change your feelings in any way, let yourself be aware of and caring toward whatever you feel."

At this point we can start to realize that *our wisdom guidance is more essential to us at these times than our challenging feelings could ever be.* How we *respond* to our feelings with our wisdom becomes our central focus rather than following the disturbed thoughts that arise out of our challenges. Our distressed feelings can become useful because they can lead us to seek our wisdom guidance, rather than following our reactive thoughts and feelings. This is a major breakthrough every time we are aware of this shift.

Key Messages

Many of us have been exposed to countless teachings and approaches to life that have told us to "Follow your feelings." This was the new age mantra for much of the sixties, seventies and eighties. For me, there was always an important caveat missing from this mantra. I believe it would serve us better if the mantra were something along the lines of "Follow your feelings *when they lead to your well-being.*"

We all know about having experiences of harmony when our hearts are open, when we are following our happiness, and when one good thing leads to another. This is what was originally meant by "Follow your feelings." But when our feelings aren't leading us to well-being, we need to have a totally different strategy in place, so that they don't rule the show and take us on a downward spiral of suffering. The new rule of thumb, I believe, needs to be: *Follow your feelings when they lead you to well-being, but absolutely follow your wisdom guidance when your feelings aren't leading to what you are most needing.*

Integrating the Chapter: Inquiries

1. When you are the angriest or most withdrawn, what is the message that you most need to listen to in order to support your life?

2. In relationships, when you are in your most distancing pattern, what is the main message that you need to hear more clearly from your wisdom guidance?

3. What are the messages from wisdom guidance that you most need to hear when you are in your most difficult emotion?

4. When you have trouble accessing your wisdom guidance, what would your friendly mind say to you to help you to stay focused on your greatest need?

For additional support and further integration of Practice Five, I strongly encourage you to listen to the guided meditations at www.AwarenessThatHeals.org.

PRACTICE SIX

Tuning into Tone of Voice

*We won't succeed in changing our tones unless we become
aware of them and are honest with ourselves.*

One of the traps we often fall into is to be focused on *what* is said to
us, or *what* we say to others. We then fail to notice *how* it is said to
us, or *how* we speak to others. While the *content* of the words is important,
the *energy and tone* behind the words are frequently even more so. When
we become aware of our tone of voice, of the nuances that shape it, and of
the impact it has in our lives, we can greatly increase our capacity to guide
our lives according to our true intentions.

The tone of voice we use communicates both our motivations and
underlying emotional state. Awareness of our tone provides insights into
what lies in our unconscious, particularly when our words and the tone in
which they are delivered are incongruent or even opposite in their message. We can more easily notice this when we are also aware of the ways
others have spoken to us.

We may say all the right and positive words from our conscious mind,
but if we are unconsciously feeling distant or critical, these feelings will

inevitably slip through in our tone and energy. Almost always, the impact of the (conscious) words will be overshadowed by the (unconscious) tone—and it is this that is often "heard" or felt by the other person, or ourselves when we're on the receiving end. Oftentimes, this is a fleeting awareness for both parties.

In this chapter, we will explore not only how you actually sound, but how you can use this awareness to improve the quality of your life. This will help you have the chance to change from a dissonant tone or energy to one that is more heartfelt.

Being aware of the impact of tone of voice—not just in our more challenging times, but in all of our interactions—is yet another entry point into understanding ourselves, and supporting intimacy and connection in our lives. It's a tool that we have at our disposal every time we are interacting with anyone.

Please don't assume that the problem with our tone of voice always means we are unconsciously "negative." It can also be a problem when we are unconsciously "positive." Either way, being *unaware* of tone of voice does not serve us—or those with whom we interact. Here is an example of what I mean.

Sarah

In every intimate relationship that Sarah decided to end, she observed how shocked each partner was by her decision. Yet she told me that she had repeatedly conveyed her dissatisfaction throughout her relationships and always told her partner when something really hurt her, and how painful it was.

"How did you tell them about your dissatisfaction? "I asked.

"Oh, I was never unkind," she said. "I was always soft, and gentle and encouraging. I didn't want them to feel like I was judging them or being too harsh."

I helped Sarah to see her double message. In tiptoeing around her partners with what she thought was kindness, she had never highlighted the depth of her distress. Her communication had always seemed too warm and tolerant to be taken seriously. And as a result, each partner had not realized the urgency of the situation until she was virtually out the door. She needed to expand the range of her tones so they reflected her deepest needs. Only in this way would she have a chance to improve her communication and have her needs met. She gradually developed the ability to express her unhappiness in part by having a congruent intensity and dissatisfaction in her tone. As a result, her relationships improved because she was expressing her depth and pain through her tone. She thus created a healthy balance to her overly kind and codependent tendencies. It also meant her partners could trust and distinguish between her disaffection and good feelings, because the two were now expressed in clearly different ways.

As a counselor, I have spent many years focusing on the impact of my own tone. Earlier in my career, I saw myself as caring—or at least neutral—almost all of the time, except with the rare client I was triggered by, and when that occurred I could belatedly hear a subtle and undesirable quality slip into my tone. As the years passed, it became apparent to me that it was more than that—I saw that I was not even *aware* of certain elements of my own tone of voice. This was particularly obvious when

I replayed from my memory what I had said out loud, which became a practice for me. At those times, I could hear (more precisely) when I was less caring.

I also understood that it is hard to hear or discern any quality unless we are able to contrast it with an alternative that we have experienced. In other words, if we are used to being professionally distant, neutral or even abrasive, it is hard to notice unless we have previously expressed ourselves in a more caring, heartfelt way or been with others who have done so.

I could see the importance of witnessing my own tone more carefully while I was with my clients. I knew that this awareness was vital and it helped me to be even more motivated to be closer to my heart. Through the years, I have heard myself at times sound somewhat self-righteous, arrogant, overbearing and impatient. On other occasions, I could be withdrawn or even slightly sarcastic. To the best of my knowledge, none of these were extreme, but they were enough to foster some disconnection from whomever I was talking with in those moments.

From these observations and explorations came the question: *Why are most of us so unaware of tone of voice?* It's clear, like so many other psychological patterns, that we need to go back and look at our origins to find out.

How We Become Tone Deaf

It can be helpful to understand why, as adults, most of us don't reliably hear tones of voice—and that includes our own and those of others. As children, most of us *were* more sensitive to the tone of others. Perhaps you remember your parents or older siblings being angry, deflated or anxious in their voice even though they claimed to be fine. At other times, for most of us, the tones of our parents would be more overt and obvious, and, when you were asked to come closer to them, you would instantly know the difference between whether you were in trouble and when you were about to receive a hug.

We have known for quite a while that many of the responses learned in early childhood are carried on into adulthood. And we know that speaking and listening patterns can become so habitual and familiar that most people aren't even aware of them. The patterns that were developed with our tone of voice are one of the most consequential of these.

When we were children, incongruent messages between the spoken word and the tone of voice inevitably caused confusion for us, because we heard one thing and experienced something very different coming toward us. Understandably, very few of us had good modeling for this, and we lost track of the value of being congruent in our tone and words. As a result, many of us became tone deaf in our childhood, losing sensitivity to inconsistencies in our own tones as well as to those which we heard from others. It was just too painful to stay that sensitive.

Below are some examples of this:

- Our parents may say to us, "Don't eat that." If they say it with disdain and shame as an ongoing message, it can create anxiety, agitation, or rebellion. They could be saying those same words out of protection and safety, but we don't experience that because of the tone they deliver it in.
- A child may be told, "Would you clean up your room." If this is said in a hostile voice, it can be enough to set up a power struggle or contribute to passive-aggressive tendencies in him or her—in some cases for a lifetime. In contrast, this could be said with a smile as a light supportive reminder, where it can be part of caring.
- The words "I miss you" could be laced with guilt and dependency, rather than a genuine expression of love that also respects independence.

- If you are told, "I'm glad you did well," from a parent who suffers from long-term depression, their somber and empty tone can make you feel like your achievements don't have value. On the contrary, it may just make you feel bad and you can't explain why. Thus we may learn not to trust validation or let in love. The same sentence, uttered with sincerity, can help us feel supported and honored.

Having worked with scores of clients on their tone of voice, I never cease to be amazed at how tender the moment is when someone awakens to its power.

Sharon

Sharon was an emotionally assertive woman with an edginess about her. An author, she was having difficulties with her agent, publishers, attorney and just about anyone who got close to her.

"I must be picking the wrong people," she told me. "They're all giving me attitude." In our first session, she used an aggressive tone to describe her attorney as "a very hard person to talk with."

"How are you experiencing your own tone of voice right now?" I asked her.

She looked puzzled, waited a moment and then said, "I guess I'm a bit frustrated, but it's understandable, given how these people have spoken to me."

I told her in a soft and sincere tone, "My experience is that you sound extremely angry. I'm wondering if you sense that as you look closer?"

Irritated at my comment, she said, "I think you're wrong and I don't know why you're judging me."

I persevered by saying, "Is that how you really feel as you listen to my tone of voice right now?" I added, "What is your sense of your tone when you're telling me I'm judging you?"

Sharon paused for a few seconds. It looked like she didn't know if she wanted to hit me or thank me. "I don't know," she finally said in an exasperated tone.

I encouraged her to reflect on what just happened as if she were in a laboratory where she could see her own reactions and hear her own tones. I explained that this kind of exploration could go a long way in helping her with all of her relationships.

"I don't know if you're right," she said in a much kinder voice, "but I appreciate your directness and I'll think about it more."

Just as Sharon, in this opening session, began to sensitize herself to her tone of voice, so each of us can begin to recognize the energy beneath the surface of our words. You can see how unaware and defensive she was about how she came across not only in the original tone, but also in being confronted with feedback by me. As the session went on, I could almost hear her shifting from tone deafness to a deeper level of listening—and healing. (We will return to Sharon later in the chapter.)

Becoming Aware of Our Own Tones

One of the times that we are most likely to miss our own tones or be unaware of them is when we feel that we have been severely wronged. When we think that our anger is justified and we resort to a pattern of blaming the other person, it renders us temporarily incapable of reaching toward healing. Simply developing curiosity about the types of tones we use in situations where our anger and other strong defensive emotions arise can be a powerful starting point for identifying our patterns of disconnecting from our heart. This can be enhanced by asking the question, "What does my tone sound like?"

It takes time and accessing awareness that heals to develop harmlessness and evenness in your tone while you're angry. At first, you're likely to find yourself somewhat resistant to this new way of responding. It can, however, be part of a significant turning point when you take the time to contemplate this practice to deepen your relationship to yourself and others.

As the following example will show, exploring the sound of our own tones and developing the capacity to hear and identify them is quite important if we want to become more sensitive and at peace with ourselves and our environment.

Charles

In the mid-1970s, two close friends and I coordinated a residential treatment center for teenagers. Charles, a member of our center, had a way of announcing his victimhood that made him stand out as a target for the other boys in the home. At the dinner table, he would attract attacks to himself by saying with a whining, high-pitched and agitated tone, "Why won't you pass me the butter?" This daily occurrence became a reliable form of "entertainment" for the other boys.

I worked with Charles for some time and his progress was

slow. He was so deeply entrenched in self-hatred, low self-esteem and anxiety, that becoming aware was difficult for him. He just thought that everyone else was mean. "After all," he said to me, "I'm not mean to anybody. I just want them to be nice to me."

For an entire year, he remained steadfast in his belief that his problems were created by other people's bad attitudes.

One day, Charles had a mini-breakthrough. I asked him to repeat the words, "Why won't you pass me the butter?" in as many different tones as possible. After several tries, he suddenly was able to speak in a more neutral tone as he said, "Pass me the butter, will you?" I heard a hint of joy in my voice as I asked him if he could hear the difference. "Yes," he said. "I wasn't nervous as I asked. I just told them what I wanted in a relaxed way."

"That's going to work," I assured him with great encouragement. "Why don't you give it a try?"

I knew that if he could sustain a neutral tone, he would be no fun to pick on any more. With several rounds of role-play, Charles got the hang of neutralizing his tone and how to relax inside at that time. After that, those kinds of attacks steadily decreased; eventually they disappeared.

This is one of the most dramatic examples of how one sentence touching the heart tone at an important moment can be a catalyst to change someone's life. Charles found a relaxed part of himself that he was able to gravitate toward that changed his relationship to the world.

Learning to Recognize Tones of Voice

Out of all the blind spots that we may have, our tone of voice is likely to be one of the most challenging to uncover and to remain aware of. The inner grooves and habits of our own tones have become so automatic and deep that we can barely, if at all, hear the tones that are not serving us. Actually, it is much easier for most of us to hear the tones in the voice of another than to deeply listen to our own.

It requires awareness, integrity and humility to be able to acknowledge the tones in your voice that are actually distancing patterns in your life and relationships. These include the tones that you use "against" yourself in your inner self-talk, as we discussed previously, as well as the hurtful tones that you convey in your relationships.

One of the primary purposes of this book is to give you strategies to allow you to experience awareness and engage a healing intention in some of your most challenging moments. Becoming aware of your tones helps you to identify the ones that cause the most suffering in your life. From there, you can engage an intention to heal and do the inner work to find heartfelt tones that are healing.

The tones that cause suffering are almost always reflections of the emotional reactions that we feel but aren't willing to say in words. And, again, this is almost always an unconscious process. Examples include tones of whining and complaining, all the way through to tones of fear, demandingness, and anger, to name a few. For many of these, we may have just a fleeting awareness that we are not very proud of our tone. When we look at how we ask for what we need in a relationship, or how we address ourselves in our minds, we often find that the way we *think* we are relating to others or ourselves is very different from how we are actually relating. The turning point is recognizing that this originates from our tone.

It's essential to understand that changing our tone isn't a cosmetic or superficial shift. It is a shift in our emotional state. We won't succeed in changing our tones unless we become aware of them and are honest with ourselves. Once we're aware they exist and that they are operating to our detriment, we need to access our awareness that heals. It is through our inner work that we cultivate our capacity to express ourselves from our hearts and to be less reactive or hurtful.

As we do this, we shift from being against the other or ourselves to finding a way to focus and access a quality that serves our well-being and that of others.

Saman

A client of mine, Saman, was incredibly surprised to learn at a corporate retreat that the team he directed thought his general management style was destructive and arrogant. At the retreat, he arranged early morning briefings with his team every day, which he thought were a good opportunity to meet and discuss the day ahead. In a supervision meeting with one of his team members, he asked him why he didn't share anything in the morning meetings. In this unusually safe setting, the team member replied, "You line us up and knock us down one by one." Saman was shocked. Up until that point he had thought his style of management and communication was very effective and supportive. But what he realized, with further corroboration, was that his very clipped and authoritarian tones of voice made his team members feel like he was condescending and that he belittled them.

This led Saman to a great deal of contemplation and eventually learning to listen to how he sounded. During one of our sessions, I asked him if I could directly mirror the sound of his voice, and he agreed. I echoed a voice that carried a tone of agitation and disdain. When he heard this tone, he was utterly flabbergasted and horrified. He had a moment of genuine insight. He said, "This is why I get so much resistance at times!"

I asked him to give me an example of what he considered to be constructive feedback. He cited something that he had recently expressed: "If you don't mind, I would like you to be more precise in the reports you give me. I have spoken to you about this several times." However, his tone was impatient, sarcastic and condescending. I asked how it sounded to him and he said "strong and constructive." I then echoed his sentences back to him. As happens almost always, he was able to hear the contrast between his tone and one that was balanced. He responded with, "Oh my," looking a bit sheepish. I let him know that I could sense his embarrassment and that this was a good sign, because it showed he was being honest, aware and cared about how he sounded.

He began to pay attention to his inner feelings and, through time and continued feedback, he learned how to soften his tone. He had to work on this for several months so that he could reliably have the awareness to differentiate between commands and requests in particular. As a result, his relationship to his whole team improved dramatically. It took his awareness, honesty and discrimination to seek a kinder place in his heart to speak with more softness and support. It wasn't merely a mechanical change in his tone—he had developed the capacity to express himself in a healing and constructive way and recognize the fact that his attitude had been, indeed, contemptuous and shaming: something he had never imagined he was capable of.

Reflection Point: Can you remember a time when someone was angry and they denied that they sounded angry, impatient or superior?

Taking It Deeper: Can you remember a time when you had an angry or frustrated tone of voice and denied it, even though at a subtle level you knew that you felt some anger?

Changing How You Speak to Yourself

Tone awareness can lead to noticing and adjusting how you speak to others, AND how you speak to yourself. When you are aware that you are at a low or angry place, one of the keys to engaging a healing tone is paying attention to how you are speaking to yourself in that moment. If you are addressing yourself in a judgmental or critical attitude, it is virtually impossible to connect to your heart and support yourself with what you need. If you continue to sense a tone of harshness, it is likely that you will need to continue to work to find your voice of balanced strength and caring.

Each of your challenging feeling tones can eventually be transformed by accessing your intention to heal—which will guide you toward different essential qualities. Once you feel more in touch with the essential qualities, you then have the capacity to project them through your tone of voice.

▼

Exercise: Next time you have a difficult moment, notice how you speak to yourself. Notice the words you use and the tones behind them. It's important to keep in mind that many times it isn't the situation that is causing the main problem for you—rather it is your interpretation of it and your reaction to the judgmental and negative tone directed toward yourself. Can you identify your most self-critical internal tones and then the situations that trigger them?

It still may be difficult to do anything about the tone once you have identified it. However, just increasing your awareness of your own tone is an accomplishment and can have a significant impact on your life.

Becoming aware of the negative tones toward yourself and others increases the chance to really make changes in your life. When you have found a more sensitive place in your heart, you can convey tones that allow for intimacy or that can replace distancing. The question that follows right on the heels of this is: "How can I do this?" In addition to using the awareness of our challenge, we need to access our intention to heal and inquiry. I also have found that many times a form of prayer can significantly help us access a purer place in our hearts.

For example, we might pray: "May I find the softest tone that will allow me to connect," or "May I find the balanced strength that will convey the importance of what I want to say without intimidating anyone." Such invocations require finding your intention to heal and applying it to your tone of voice when you realize it has been, or is, harsh or frightened. As you progress with this work you will begin to notice the impact this has. You'll be given other tools in the next couple of practices too.

Tones Don't Lie

How many times in your life has your trust diminished for someone when they said the right words but their words didn't feel genuine? Much of the authenticity that you may be seeking in others comes from their tone.

When our words are not communicating what's really in our heart, our tone of voice will reveal it clearly to those who are listening carefully. Conversely, when we are congruent and our tone reflects our truth, people will naturally connect with our meaning.

When speaking with my clients about their wish to express caring even though they feel empty or withdrawn, they are often concerned that they come off as phony or inauthentic. I often suggest the Alcoholics Anonymous adage: "Sometimes you have to fake it till you make it." This means that you might express the intention to be more kind, but not be able to carry it out in action at first. However, as you deepen your commitment to yourself and your practice, you will become more adept at finding a tone that naturally reflects your intention. The rewards are immense.

Here are some examples of exploring tone with awareness:

- We may tell a friend that we are okay with their persistent lateness because we want to sound accepting. But if we listen closely to our tone, we might hear discontentment or annoyance, which reveals our underlying unhappiness.
- We may have an understanding with our partner that each of us will take on certain responsibilities and/or respect each other's wishes in various ways. When our partner fails to fulfill his or her

commitment, we may *say* that we are fine with it and use words like "Uh huh" or "I understand." However, if we listen to our *tone*, we will hear ambivalence, resignation, disappointment or even anger.

- We may act like we're okay when our lover frequently avoids intimate contact, but we are aware of a tone we either express or internalize that contains vulnerability, defensiveness or withdrawal.

Checking Out Our Own Tone First

If we want to involve someone else in this exploration of tone of voice, we first need to be aware of our own tone. Have you ever heard a parent or a teacher confronting a child for the judgmental way they are speaking, while at the same time employing a tone that's even harsher and more negative? If there is tension or tightness in our own voice when we reflect someone else's tone to them, it will only create more resistance and separation. We can only effectively talk about someone else's tone when our own is relaxed or at least neutral. Paradoxically, even when we're right about the substance of a situation, our tone can be so off that it, then, becomes the bigger issue.

When you're alone, take a look at your closest and most challenging relationships and contemplate which discordant tones of voice you are most likely to express to each person. You could then ask, "In each relationship, what qualities do I need to support and express to help heal my tone?" Your wisdom guidance might say, "Remember to be open to as much kindness, sensitivity and empathy as possible." Contemplating your tone, when you are away from the heat of the moment, is one of the best methods of supporting greater intimacy and heart in your life.

Over the years, I have observed countless couples and the tone they use with one another. Most of the time when there is a relationship conflict, their tone of voice reflects it and is often a central part of it. And as I guide couples to work with their tone, we go right to the source of what is causing the injury. This allows them to experience a tremendous healing.

This healing can also occur in business or in any personal relationship. Maybe our reactivity is triggered when one of our challenging business associates is lecturing us with condescension. In a belittling tone, they may say, "Is it too much to ask for you to pay closer attention to what you are doing?" Perhaps we respond with either an aggressive or distant tone. What usually follows is an unintended escalation. When we develop the ability to hear and become accountable for how our reactivity is expressing itself through our own tone of voice, we will also develop the sensitivity to recognize an issue before it can escalate. We can use our awareness to shift from blindly replying, to finding and accessing our healing tones and words to change the flow of the conversation.

When working with our tone of voice in relationships, we need to consider several things in order to be effective. First, we need to reflect on our own tone, and check if we are in a frame of mind to be friendly or, at the very least, neutral. When we see that we aren't, we need to be honest with ourselves, and access an intention to heal and contemplate what the quality is that we want to express in our voice. Finally, before entering into a potentially challenging conversation centered specifically on our own or the other's tone, we have to make sure to be attentive to whether they are receptive or not. There is no point in having a one-way conversation or one where the other feels coerced or trapped into it.

▼

Reflection Point: Do you remember a time when you felt severely wronged and your tone of voice was angry or defensive in some way? Even though you may have felt that the person got what they deserved, can you imagine hearing a specific tone that would have given a chance of greater connection?

Taking It Deeper: Do you remember a time when you were on the receiving end of a tone of voice that was angry? As you look back, did it seem like the person involved felt like they had been wronged? Imagine yourself taking an interest in what they really wanted or needed that made them mad in the first place. Let yourself focus on your response with a tone that you'd like to receive if you were in their shoes.

Asking Permission

When you want to enter into a conversation which concerns another person's tone of voice, again, as highlighted, you need to first reflect on your own emotional state. When you have strong feelings, and know that you are likely to express them, it is essential to ask the other's permission first. This gives them time to adjust and be as receptive as possible. In fact, this actually can, in many cases, de-escalate the feelings. And when you do ask for permission, and get it, remember that you are entering high-risk territory. You need to be ready to drop the situation and re-approach it when the feelings are not so charged.

Asking permission is only going to work if you have at least a neutral or caring tone *as you do so*. Come from a sincere place inside yourself because it will increase the chances that your response will be well received. You will almost certainly lessen the chance that the conversation could escalate in a negative way.

If you have both agreed to explore your tones together, it is vital that you each look for as relaxed a tone as possible and set it up so you can agree to disagree with your perceptions and views. Your main focus needs to be on ensuring that you both make your best effort to express a healing tone as you deal with your disagreement.

This practice requires awareness and the dedication to try and try again if necessary. A prerequisite is that you access awareness that heals to guide you, both before and during any attempt. From my experience, these are times when we are much more likely to be overly trusting of our own tone and not be aware of a subtle resistance or anger we may have. When we can let this likelihood in, it allows for some humility, which can soften our anger or aggression.

Remember that, when it comes to relationships, we are often repeating years of distorted tones (accusatory, victimized, overly positive, etc.) that we have been taught and modeled, not only by our parents, but also by society in general. It takes courage, honesty and persistence to unravel these patterns and to consistently address them in a supportive way.

Reflection Point: Pause for a moment and focus your attention inwards. Ask yourself what one or two of your most challenging tones are, as you look over the people in your everyday life. The tone will most likely be connected with a person who is difficult for you to interact with or who triggers you intensely at certain times. See if you can describe the feelings.

Taking It Deeper: As you recall these tones, inquire and look for the tones that are healing. Take some time to ground yourself in your intention to heal and to sense how these healing tones feel. Speak them out loud or hear yourself as if you are listening to a tape recording. If you are able to hear the quality desired, can you see the likely difference in outcome in the situations you faced and will face if you are able to evolve with your more open-hearted tones?

As you aspire to make your tone of voice more consistent with your intentions, sometimes it will be difficult or even impossible. These are the times where your friendly mind can come in to support you. It will say something like, "I realize how difficult this is for you. Stay focused: it's okay if it takes a period of time before you can come close to even feeling the tone. Wait until you are ready before you try to express yourself." If we seek our friendly mind's support, our chances of persevering exponentially increase.

Reflecting on What Disturbs You

It may help you understand tone of voice more personally if you think about what disturbs or triggers you. If you bring to mind people with whom you have had a conflict and then hone in on their tone of voice, chances are that a major part of the issue stemmed from the way they spoke to you or at least how you heard them. If this is the case, what tone in their voice made you most reactive?

This chart contains a partial list of common emotional reactions that can be triggering. Which are the ones that you have the greatest aversion toward?

arrogance	lecturing	praising
control	superiority	anxiety
excessive validation	helplessness	emptiness
intimidation	despair	irritation
wounding	depression	melodrama
domination	seriousness	anger

Reflection Point: From this chart, what are the tones of voice, either from you or someone else, that frequently cause the most suffering in your life? In your present or past love relationships, what tones have been the most difficult for you?

Taking It Deeper: Let your awareness focus on what your most defensive or distant tones of voice sound like when you feel wronged or misunderstood. Then contemplate what tonal qualities you would aspire to experience and express that would bring you toward harmony and healing. Again, don't forget you will likely need your friendly mind to support your empathy, patience and perseverance.

My client Sharon, who appeared early on in this chapter, had just begun to be aware of her aggressive tone of voice. In her next session, she told me that she realized she had a major "attitude," just like the people who were troubling her. This was a huge breakthrough. Over the next several months, she recognized that for the rest of her life, she needed to stay aware of her tone of voice. She said, "I can see that my tone has been a major contributor to the problems in each of my relationships."

She even acknowledged that in some relationships, she was the initiator. She said she knew that I appreciated her strength, because she could feel it in my attitude and tone of voice. In fact, my lack of reactivity, when she was acting her anger out, gave her the space to really tune in and feel herself. Sharon was internalizing some of the tone of kindness, and she felt the beginnings of compassion toward herself for having felt the need to act out so much anger, and then deal with the unhappy consequences.

In one of our last sessions, she said quite tenderly, "I can see why I've needed to use my anger so much. It was the only way I could defend myself when I was young." She smiled with a knowing sadness. "I just spent thirty years before I realized I don't have to do it this way anymore."

Key Messages

Our tones, whether we're aware of them or not, truly reveal the attitudes and qualities that we put forth in the world as well as those we experience inside ourselves. It is hard to imagine a better way to read what's in our hearts and souls than listening to the music expressed through our tones.

To glimpse and then develop our ability to hear our major unpleasant tones reflects emotional sensitivity and honesty. It is a concrete way to work on our own development that is likely to be both humbling and inspiring. How else could it reflect the full range of human experience if it didn't cover the best and most challenging parts inside us projected outwardly in sound?

Integrating the Chapter: Inquiries

1. What is the tone of voice that you have the hardest time acknowledging and being accountable for?
2. What tone of voice of yours causes the most pain in you or others? And when you're in touch with an intention to heal, what qualities would be most helpful during these times?
3. What tone of voice are you the most reactive toward, and what tone would be easier to hear? Can you see yourself asking for the tone you need?
4. What qualities are most important for you to develop in support of regulating and harmonizing your tone of voice in a healing way? Please don't forget the **Introspective Guides**: they are of immense help in identifying the qualities.

For additional support and further integration of Practice Six, I strongly encourage you to listen to the guided meditations at www.AwarenessThatHeals.org.

Moving from Feelings to Needs

It is important for you to inquire and find guidance to help you to make the connection between your challenging feelings and the needs that will best take care of them.

All of the practices so far have prepared us to embrace the awareness of our current challenging feelings as a vehicle to directly discover what we need in order to take optimal care of ourselves and those we love. Now we can tap into one of our most precious resources: our capacity to identify and connect with the needs that lie *just beneath the surface* of our disturbing feelings and circumstances.

When we are challenged emotionally, we can uncover the direct, positive connection between what we feel and what we need. Most importantly, we recognize that this healing connection can be made for our own well-being.

Our emotional suffering is often a result of thwarted desires or needs. At these times, we invariably experience critical or negative thoughts and emotions. We don't usually recognize the potentially healing link between our suffering and the fact that we wanted something that didn't turn out the way we hoped. We often circle around the same thought, or a variation of it, for hours, days and sometimes weeks or more. We fail to recognize that it was our unmet desires or needs that triggered the challenging feeling in the first place.

When I talk about needs, I am not referring to survival needs such as food, shelter, water and air, nor am I addressing needs that arise from medical, chemical, hormonal or genetic causes. Instead, I use the word *need* to describe essential qualities that I have referred to previously, such as compassion, tenderness, strength, courage, love of the truth and peace.

Whenever one of your essential needs is not being met, you suffer—and that suffering can reveal your need. Here are some examples:

- If you feel guilty, you have a need for innocence.
- If you feel afraid, you have a need for courage or safety—or both.
- If you feel empty, you have an unmet need for aliveness or fulfillment.
- If you feel hurt, you have a need for comfort or soothing.

The point is not to deny or "get over" the feeling. At this juncture you want to support yourself by focusing on caring for your feelings and contemplating your unmet needs so you can work toward getting them met.

Why do difficult emotions exist in the first place? And why do they often grab center stage in our lives?

Almost always these feelings exist because the core needs that lie *underneath* them have been thwarted. Our feelings, then, provide vital information about what we want and need.

This understanding, when utilized, supports us no matter what we are feeling and will lead us to our most essential and wholesome healing qualities. When we've identified what we need in our relationships, we can learn to express and take care of that need. Our feelings guide us to that need and we can then take healing, helpful action—for ourselves, and for others.

Forging the Healing Link Between Feelings and Needs

Our emotions can be so riveting, so powerful, and so compelling that, without the practices, our needs often remain not only unmet, but also invisible. Our feelings literally hide our underlying needs from our sight. Anxiety, anger and other emotions can blind us with their intensity. *We are not aware we have these essential needs because we are distracted by the emotions that, paradoxically, are one of the important reasons our needs remain unmet.* Most of us live our lives without being aware of this circular bind we're in.

The link between our feelings and needs is a master key to our healing and growth. To make good use of this key, from now on, when you are experiencing a difficult emotion, you can be on the alert to access your intention to care for yourself so that you can identify the underlying need. For example, if you felt sad, what was it you wanted that would have made you happy? If you felt frightened, what did you need that would have allowed you to feel safe or courageous?

Once you see this connection, the potential is there for any challenge you feel to become a pathway to discovering your essential needs and qualities. The more you do this, the more your needs will take center stage, rather than your feelings. As you use this practice and access the connection between your feelings and needs, your trust and confidence in finding your needs builds, and the fear of being trapped in challenges is reduced or eliminated.

From Challenging Feelings to Essential Qualities and Needs Sequences

Chart Two, in the **Introspective Guides** (also available for download at www.AwarenessThatHeals.org), has almost the same title as this section: I encourage you to use it as we work together. It is designed to guide you not only through this chapter, but also your life when any challenging times arise. Each line begins with a common challenging emotion, followed by a sequence of healing qualities that you can use to help you move toward greater healing.

As you go deeper into the practice, you will likely experience an increased respect for all your emotions—even the ones that are injurious—because you become aware of how they can guide you toward your needs. We, and everyone around us, benefit when we look for and find our essential needs and qualities.

Stephen

A client of mine, Stephen, had suffered intermittently for many years from a low-level feeling of emptiness, apathy and a lack of motivation. As he became more aware of this during our sessions, he realized that these experiences of feeling empty were becoming more frequent and more serious. While he had taught himself to cope with them fairly well, he also wondered, "Am I doing everything I can?"

With this awareness, he realized that he hadn't been very kind toward himself. His inquiry had a message that sounded like, "Why don't you know what you want? What's wrong with you? You're depressed and not lovable."

Over time, he made the crucial pivot from hearing self-critical questions to accessing his friendly mind. "It's okay that you feel empty and it's great you've learned that there is a way to support it, rather than judging it."

Gradually the deeper needs beneath the emptiness emerged: Stephen wanted more depth, intimacy and heart-to-heart communication in his love life and friendships. He found a growing tolerance and compassion for his yearning. It began to feel more like a companion than an enemy. Slowly his emptiness warmed, softened and began to reveal its true wish: a reaching out for authentic connection, meaning and love. This led him to share his inner experience with all of the richness of his feelings and needs that were most important to him with those he most trusted, and to be more empathically interested in those closest to him. He realized experientially that by facing his major challenges in this way, his life was gradually becoming more fulfilled.

The Distinction between Desires and Needs

One more distinction that is important to highlight is the difference between desires and needs. Desires, in the way I am using that word, are mostly focused on pleasures and enjoyments. They can be for travel, food, success or entertainment; but they can only go so deep—while our essential needs, as we have been exploring, live in our hearts and represent our deepest fulfillment.

At the same time, because desires are prominent in our lives, we have to be aware of the challenging emotions that usually arise when they are thwarted: it's similar to the way we feel when our essential needs are blocked. Although desires aren't our primary focus in this book, seeing how they can affect us emotionally can lead us to address and support our deeper needs. It helps to know whether we are upset because a desire is being blocked or because an essential need is not being met. When we can distinguish between the two, we can respond with discernment: when it is a desire, almost invariably we need to grow in our capacity to let go. The practice we are exploring in this chapter will help you to do just that.

There are also desires that aren't focused on just pleasure and enjoyment. Many of us are fixated on desires in life that are impossible to fulfill, and these inevitably lead us to confusing and challenging feelings.

Here are some common examples:

- I wish I'd had a different childhood.
- I want my lover to be more attractive and more intelligent.
- I want my partner to be more developed than they are in an area that isn't viable or desired on their part.
- I want my political party to be in power now, when it isn't.
- I want the weather to be more beautiful than it is today.
- I want to have a more powerful car but I can't afford it.
- I want to be thinner than I am, even though I've been doing all that I can.
- I don't want to feel sick when I am sick.
- I want more money than I have right now.
- I want my family to love me more than they do.
- I want my favorite sports team to win.

Reflection Point: Contemplate the desire that has created the most suffering for you throughout your life. See if you can notice how much it can take control of you and cause you to feel disturbed. (Refer to the just-mentioned examples of desires that are impossible to fulfill, if nothing comes to your mind.)

Taking It Deeper: Taking this same desire, explore how you can work with yourself to relax with it and/or support letting it go.

Uncovering the Deeper Needs behind Our Emotions

When our unmet needs create challenging emotions, our lack of awareness often leads us to either withdraw from, or take our feelings out on, someone else. These outcomes are symptoms of not being able to identify our challenging emotions and not being in touch with our intention to heal. *Identifying the link between our feelings and these core needs is an essential part of our growth and fulfillment.* Seeing how our challenging feelings are correlated to our specific needs is crucial; it is a gateway to more connection and intimacy.

It is important for you to inquire and find guidance to help you to make the connection between your feelings and your unmet essential needs. Your inquiry needs to be affirming and phrased in a way you can see is realistic in the current moment or in the near future. An example of this is "What is the most important need to support that will allow me to best take care of myself in the next few minutes?"

Here is the healing sequence.

Awareness > Intention to Heal > Inquiry > Essential Needs

As you read the following scenarios, see if you can identify where awareness, intention to care for yourself, inquiry and then essential needs come into play. I ask you to do that because first: it is so important to see how the process itself works and second: once you've integrated the process, you can make it conscious and relatable so you can make the practice your own.

- Cecile felt hurt by her lover, but wanted to find a way to be closer. This led her to ask herself, "What is it that I need?" After some contemplation, she saw that she needed a gentler tone and more frequent touch to soothe her. She felt that if she could communicate this in a constructive way, it would be worth the attempt to have a conversation.

- Bruce felt rejected because his friend Peter had not reached out to him in months. This led him to pause and reflect, which put him in touch with both his need for more contact as well as the loss he experienced without it. Bruce asked himself, "How can I best convey my feelings to Peter? I want to find the right amount of contact that works for both of us." Bruce didn't want to express any blame or pressure and imagined saying something like, "I don't want to put any pressure on you, Peter, but I would really appreciate it if you could tell me if you would like to have more space in our friendship or whether something else is going on that has stopped you from contacting me. My experience is that I have been the one to call or email you first for quite a while, and I want to hear about how you see this and hear what would work best for you."

- Jane felt terrible physically. She contemplated the question, "What ways can I eat, exercise, or otherwise give myself the best chance to feel better?" She made a commitment to herself that if she saw anything she could do, then she would act on it, knowing it was an expression of self-love. Jane also allowed herself the freedom and flexibility that if she didn't see anything she could do, she would say gently to herself, "Relax and stay open to what might help your situation and yourself."

Reflection Point: Identify a past situation that happened with a friend when you felt treated insensitively, and you wanted to be treated with more kindness but didn't share it. Can you remember why? Some reasons could have been that you felt too vulnerable to being criticized, or that you wouldn't be received well. Perhaps you were afraid the other person wouldn't be receptive enough to give you an honest answer.

Taking It Deeper: Reflect upon the same situation as above and let yourself identify with the need that you had as clearly as you can. Envision yourself expressing this need to your friend in the tone that would maximize the chance of being heard. Remember to express it with both words and tone that are positive.

It is always helpful to look at your greatest need in practical and present terms. That way, you won't get lost in conceptually thinking about something that doesn't exist in the present or near future, where you have no realistic chance to make your situation better.

Here are some questions you can keep asking yourself to help you find your way to your needs:

- What do I need to do now? What attitude do I want to focus on that will help me the most in the situation I find myself?
- When I look around me at what's happening right now and discover a need, I can ask, "Is this the right time to act on what I'm needing?"
- Is this a desire that I need to let go of?
- Do I need to find this healing inside myself or is it outside?

If you engage in these questions often, you will find the clarity and precise intelligence that will help guide you to what you need and give you the best chance to fulfill it. You might require outside help to reach a state of contentment or peace. A counselor, friend, lover or family member may treat you with that kindness, empathy, acceptance or tolerance that you need as they express their appreciation for you. Oftentimes it is easier to receive from another than from yourself.

And right now, I want to again put forth this important reminder: Awareness of a quality isn't sufficient on its own. You need to take that next step of reaching inside to access your intention to heal or care for yourself. It is only when you engage that intention, whether through thought or accessing a quality and/or action, that you are truly initiating the healing process.

Healing Our Vulnerable Feelings

As we become aware of our vulnerable, or softer, feelings, we can access our intention to heal, and then identify and move toward our needs. In Practice Eight we will focus on resistant emotions that have some element of fight in them. Here we are going to zero in on caring for our own vulnerable feelings. I have found through extensive experience with my clients that the steps are not always easy to see. And they are ever so important. With that in mind, I've used the next examples and a case study to clearly identify the steps so that you can see how you can apply this to your own life.

Example #1:

Awareness > Intention to Heal > Curiosity > Acceptance

You notice a feeling of pain or sadness when you are visiting your family. (Awareness) You wonder about what you need for yourself. You contemplate and realize that you would really like to share more kindness and curiosity (Intention to Heal) toward them and hopefully receive something similar in return. You also see that this requires you to observe each family member independently to learn what is optimal and natural for each person.

You start with simple and non-threatening questions with your family based on what areas have been most comfortable in the past, such as "What's been happening in your life these days?" You attempt to take the conversation one step deeper than it has been when you get a positive response. You continue, "Are you enjoying the work that you are doing?" "How do you feel about what's happening in the world?" "What has been most interesting or inspiring to you?" (Curiosity)

When there is receptivity, you might continue trying to go to a deeper level. However, be careful not to step over the line or be invasive. It's normal and true in all explorations of new territory, that you may go too far once or twice—and when that happens, you back off and, if it feels appropriate, try again later on. It's almost always beneficial to enter a friendly, non-threatening conversation about the world, business, or whatever is comfortable to support peace and relaxation.

Communication at a level that isn't deep may or may not be exactly what you want. Be that as it may, when it comes to family, where relationships are built into our lives in a way that is predetermined, learning to enjoy being with our close relations and creating mutual ease is the only sensible way to go. (Acceptance)

Example #2:

Awareness > Intention to Heal > Accountability > Acceptance

I'd felt depleted from an ongoing illness and barely had the energy to call my doctor. I made an attempt and I was told he would get to me with the rest of his calls at the end of the day. But I knew if he called then, I'd miss the timing for getting refills of my important medications. I was aware of feeling helpless and I started looking for a way to help myself, at least for the afternoon, until I had a chance of hearing from the doctor. I realized that I didn't want to go to an emergency room, as the amount of money it would cost wasn't worth the small risk of consequences.

I found myself getting defensively angry with my doctor's unavailability (Awareness), but heard my wisdom guidance saying to me, "I hear that you feel helpless and you're afraid that this will lead to major consequences. But realistically you'll make your best efforts and be okay even if you do miss a day and have to continue feeling sick as a result. I can also see that you feel a bit guilty, for waiting until the last day to order the medications, and there's no point in blaming yourself now. (Awareness) Let this be a reminder for the future to order your medication ahead of time. Relax and breathe as much as possible—you can tolerate feeling guilty, especially in light of your commitment to take better care of your fear and being accountable in the future." (Intention to Heal and Accountability) I felt a sigh of relief as I anticipated trusting in my dedication to take better care of myself going forward. (Trust)

Healing Long-term, Chronic Feelings

In addition to these transitory vulnerable feelings, there are also the vulnerable feelings that are more sustained and become long-term, chronic patterns.

When a challenge is "chronic," I mean that it can almost always be traced to an inner emotional pattern that has been lifelong. It manifests in repetitive ways in relationships, friendships, family intimacy, work or our inner emotional experience of life.

As I mentioned, our chronic situations almost always require a lot more time and patience in order for us to experience any kind of deep healing. You may find yourself unable to tolerate a deep shame, which will require giving yourself ongoing self-compassion and self-love for healing. You will likely need to spend a significant amount of time in stages of stabilizing awareness, intention to heal, tolerance and acceptance before you can even contemplate anything close to true self-love. I want to re-iterate that the focus here is not on the end result of self-love; nor does it include the belief that nothing has been achieved until you reach the ultimate healing. Instead, the focus is on deeply appreciating every step you take on the path of healing.

Please note that in each of the following examples, the initial challenging feeling will almost always have the most intensity relative to the healing quality that is needed. As has been emphasized, this is because our most challenging lifelong feelings were felt from our infancy on a primal level. The essential qualities that you are developing are unfamiliar

- 187 -

compared to the feelings you have had for your whole life.

As is the case with shorter-term challenges, we still need to find our way to awaken and spark our intention to heal and care for ourselves. We will also need to be able to tolerate the difficult emotion, and then go through the sequence of qualities with increasing self-compassion to bring ourselves to genuine healing. Having patience at this point can be challenging, as we so much want to be able to feel good as soon as possible. Here your friendly mind can create such important benefits. It will always say something like, "I'm sorry you have to go through this, but it is natural that it will take time to be able to feel what would be most relieving or fulfilling."

Example #1:

Awareness > Intention to Heal > Vulnerability > Discipline > Independence

A client of mine, Anna, recognized that her adult son suffered from guilt and shame over his dependence on her. (Awareness) John had been diagnosed with ADD and was ashamed of his own feelings of failure in school and work. He had been unemployed for years and could not find any motivation to move forward. He preferred living at home and playing video games and let that absorb his attention in order to escape his feelings. Anna had an enormous wish to motivate him and to support his healing (Intention to Heal), and through our sessions she realized that she was actually taking too much responsibility for him.

They had many power struggles and she recognized that trying to motivate him wasn't working. She would ask John, with a tinge of frustration, to look on the Internet for job opportunities or to walk by stores to look for signs of jobs being offered. He would reply with anger, "Alright Mom, stop bugging me! I heard you and you don't have to tell me over and over!" This would occur even though Anna was being very careful not to nag or provoke him. He continued to play video games and would say, without credibility, when she came home, "I looked at a few jobs on the computer, but they didn't look right for me." Whenever she tried to ask him what his strategy was, those were fighting words for him.

Anna eventually realized that the best hope was to share her more vulnerable feelings of helplessness and fear with him. She told him she knew it was up to him and she let him know in a sensitive way that she felt helpless and frightened. (Vulnerability) At first this disoriented him and then he began focus on himself. He stopped resisting her as much: a door had been opened for him to face how deeply dependent he was. He started to feel his own feelings of inadequacy and shame and to show this vulnerability in their conversations.

This awareness catalyzed a desire to take care of himself instead of lashing out at her. (Intention to Heal) Anna's sharing of her helplessness helped him find his own. Her longing and prayers for him to be able to find a way to do this (and the fact that she was not letting her frustration get in the way) touched him and activated him to start looking at himself.

John realized he needed to give up some of his pleasurable desires as he began to see how he had been sabotaging his life by indulging them. He started to summon up the discipline needed, and this was supported by mutually vulnerable conversations with Anna. (Discipline) He started to search for employment. After failing at a couple of jobs that he hated, he found a job with Lyft and felt really at home there.

John was on his way to finding a new kind of independence both emotionally and practically, after years of being caught in shame, frustration and power struggles. (Independence)

Example #2:
Awareness > Intention to Heal > Tolerance > Trust >
Self-Compassion

Julie was a very bright and attractive young woman who came to therapy fully expecting *not* be understood. She took one look at me and said, "I know you are just going to tell me that I'm crazy to feel unhappy. I have what everyone wants: looks, money and brains, so how could I possibly be sad? I don't even understand it myself, but I'm even having some repeated thoughts about suicide a lot these days because I feel so depressed." (Awareness)

My first concern was to explore and conclude that Julie wasn't seriously considering suicide. I thanked her for being so open. It touched my heart, as it always does, to have someone be so transparent and direct. She was confused when I thanked her, and I let her know that most people who come in have a persona that they hide behind.

It became clear, as Julie described her childhood feelings and relationship to her parents, that her depression was not a chemical or genetic condition. It had started in her late teens and she had never talked about it openly with anyone. This was her first experience of therapy. I told her that I wanted to be part of her healing team, but she would have to look inward to find the source of her suffering. She said, "I really have never felt supported, and I want to do whatever I have to do in order to heal." (Intention to Heal)

I asked her, "How hard is it for you to be okay with these feelings of depression?" She said, "It's almost impossible and I can just barely tolerate it." (Tolerance) I let her know how important tolerance was, and that together we would support her to feel the way she did openly whenever she was in a safe space to do so. In addition, she could use her energy to take care of herself, rather than being drained by thinking she was crazy. The relief was palpable, as she realized that she didn't have to perform at being a good client and that she didn't have to make the depression go away. "Whenever you can, have the courage and humility to just be as you are, and see if you can say anything at all supportive to yourself," I suggested to her after a few sessions. This was the beginning of her starting to use her friendly mind.

Through time, Julie was able to relax more and more, and instead of being predominantly critical toward herself and overly concerned about how she was being seen, she began to understand that developing her tolerance and kindness toward herself was a crucial piece of her healing. She was able to develop an inner dialogue coming from her kindness that said, "I know you're not being depressed on purpose. I am here with you and am sending you a great wish for ease and acceptance."

As she reflected on her life, she was able to see that she had been driven to be successful, attractive and sexy, but had learned nothing about vulnerability, communication and self-caring. Throughout life she had treated herself like an object. She developed the ability to consistently inquire, "What do I really need?" She noticed how different she felt when she was being open, communicative and inquiring into what might support her. "This combination is a big part of what I need, yet I have had no one that I have ever really shared myself with, including myself," she said with a smile. "I have always presented myself as this package," she told me. (This is a much more common pattern than you might think, as we were all brought up in a culture that reinforces these ideals.) She also shared with me that the **Introspective Guides** helped her to see her needs and feelings much more clearly.

The depth of her depression significantly decreased over the next few years, and she even experienced some sense of lightness during this stage, particularly in our sessions together. Julie realized that she wanted to bring the qualities that she had discovered into her outer world, but felt a deep sense of despair as she really didn't know where to start. She asked herself a series of questions such as, "What do I need to feel good today?" "What do I need to feel satisfied with my life?" "How do I bring healing to this sadness?" "How can I relate to others in a way that will be of benefit and healing to them?"

Julie met someone and quite early in the relationship emphasized that her top priorities were communication and sensitivity. He didn't understand what she meant; he thought he was already a good communicator and wasn't open to new ways to improve, so it didn't work out. After several unsatisfying experiences with other men, she met someone that was attracted to her depth. She was on her way to developing new ways of relating to herself and others. It was an enormous change from what had been an almost constant state of depression to now fluctuating between that state and a sense of trust. (Trust) Julie still had feelings of emptiness and sadness, but instead of it consuming her, she became trusting enough to get into the give and take of sharing and caring for these parts of herself. She accepted it as natural in a love relationship and felt a new love toward herself. (Self-Compassion) It took a period of about five years to make the change, and for her, every step on the way was worth it.

Example #3:

Awareness > Intention to Heal > Contemplation >

Discrimination > Acceptance

Brett was aware of feeling helpless because he had asked Edward numerous times for the same need, which was that he touch him more affectionately and sensitively during foreplay. (Awareness) Even though there had been no response up to then, Brett knew he felt both love and loved beyond what he had ever experienced, and he wanted to find a place inside himself that could continue to love Edward even if he couldn't communicate on this subject. (Intention to Heal)

Brett saw that there were so many other ways that Edward loved him and that this particular piece was only a small fraction of what was essential to him. (Contemplation and Discrimination) He knew that he would continue to ask through time and maybe even go to counseling if his perspective changed. At that point, however, he had found enough peace knowing that he could stay focused on the big picture to soften his heart and let go with his mind. Sometimes he dealt with it himself by going inside, broadening his perspective and allowing a shift in his feeling. Occasionally, as they were holding and hugging each other, he was able to make a subtle shift without talking about it, and things were gradually changing. (Acceptance)

▼

Reflection Point: Using Chart Two, **From Challenging Feelings to Essential Qualities and Needs,** identify one chronic situation or challenging feeling that you have been dealing with for a long time. Reflect on what would give you the best chance for healing. See if you can find your awareness of the challenge and identify the first quality that you would need to begin the process of healing.

Taking It Deeper: Reflect upon the quality you chose and where you are in your evolution. Let your awareness glimpse the next qualities that you see yourself needing even though you can't feel them yet. See if you can use your friendly mind to encourage you to stay focused on caring for yourself both in the present and the near future if you can't feel what you need to yet.

Remember that your path to healing is going to be unique to you, and it might take some experimenting to be clear which qualities are the ones that are right for you in this situation.

Key Messages

Our awareness of whatever emotion is challenging to us is so central. I highlight this because it is the catalyst for the healing potential that we all have. With this awareness, the powerful aspiration to care for ourselves then and there is naturally triggered—it is a breakthrough every time we are able to have these two occur simultaneously. We are able to clearly see the connection between what we feel and what we need, and the questions that follow as to how this is most viable are naturally inspired.

There is always a potentially healing question you can ask yourself when you have a challenging feeling, situation or even thought. The question could be something like, "What is it that I really need that will be helpful or healing now?" As intuitively obvious as this may sound, in the heat of a moment, most of us forget to ask this when it matters the most. To make it as much of an automatic response as possible, it is important that you create a sentence for yourself that frames a healing question or inquiry, and that you keep it in mind. The question can be a dependable launching point in diverse circumstances as long as it genuinely sparks your interest for what you need. The **Underlying Needs/Essential Qualities** chart will give you a clear presentation of the wide variety of needs we all have. It will be an invaluable aid not only in the present, but also at any time when life challenges you the most.

Integrating the Chapter: Inquiries

1. In your love relationships (past or present), what challenging feelings come to the forefront? What are the needs and qualities that would help most to take care of those feelings?
2. What qualities or needs do you most lack in your life, and what message is your wisdom guidance suggesting to you to maximize your potential?
3. What do you most need to say to yourself when you are in your greatest challenging feelings today or this week?
4. What desire do you have that creates the most challenges for you?

For additional support and further integration of Practice Seven, I strongly encourage you to listen to the guided meditations at www.AwarenessThatHeals.org.

Transforming Anger into Intimacy and Strength

If we can bring awareness that heals to our anger, we can learn how to passionately go for what we need instead of continuing to fight what we're against.

*A*nger—how do *you* handle it?

Do you express it—or suppress it? Do you "dump it"—or "stuff" it? Of course, either way you might not recognize how often it happens to you—or how deeply it affects you.

Either of these approaches inevitably creates harm sooner or later. I have found a third alternative that, I believe, is much more healing. You can *contain anger in a way that supports experiencing the feelings fully and safely—and this opens the door to the discovery and pursuit of what you truly need.* In this chapter we will explore the concept of containment in detail. I will also share with you a seven-step process that can make a significant difference in how you handle anger—and how this can empower many parts of your life.

For virtually all of us, it is extremely hard to see anger as an integral part of our own healing. We tend to consider anger, and its related feelings of outrage and aggressiveness, as a problem, not a resource. This isn't surprising since most of us have experienced anger as injurious—the opposite of healing.

The expression and even the acknowledgment of anger are seen as taboo in much of our society. As a result, we aren't given the tools or strategies to handle it effectively, and all too often it ends up being expressed or experienced in ways that are injurious. When we are angry, it is usually because we feel something important to us has not gone our way. I have found that if we're willing to genuinely look for what really disturbs us, anger can lead to an important revelation of what truly matters deep within us. Viewing anger in this light can lead us to the unmet needs or desires that reside underneath it.

How can we support ourselves to feel anger *safely*? This chapter is an exploration of a new way of experiencing anger and resistant emotions. This includes recognizing the vulnerability and underlying need contained in them. Learning how to use our anger as a catalyst for healing, rather than allowing it to be a destructive force, is an opportunity for creating a new capacity for intimacy and strength. This is a safe way of experiencing and expressing strong feelings, and it means we don't dump them on others. It is a way to apply awareness that heals to one of the most challenging areas—and explosive emotions—of our lives.

Anger is one of many challenging and resistant emotions or feelings. As was mentioned in Practice Seven, vulnerable emotions are also challenging; but what I call *resistant* feelings challenge us in an entirely different way. These emotions, which include resentment, bitterness, frustration, impatience, judgment, etc., hold within them some form of "being *against* something or someone." We experience them as contracting, negative or having an element of fight in them: they are the ones that most commonly create injury to others, and uptightness in ourselves. As we focus on our resistant emotions, you'll discover ways to redirect them toward healing instead.

Reflection Point: What is the most common resistant emotion that you feel that has most often kept you at a distance from others?

Taking It Deeper: Can you remember the last time you expressed this feeling? If so, how did you feel about the outcome?

Many of us believe that we don't have a significant issue with our awareness of anger and the way we handle our expression of it. But even so, our anger still, even if unintentional, often hurts ourselves and others. This is because we have not learned how to contemplate and support our anger in a way that allows us to wake ourselves up to our vulnerability and lead us to what we need. When we are angry, we can often intellectually see our anger is rising, but if our intention to care for ourselves has not been engaged, an ongoing cycle of pain is created. At these times we haven't yet seen that our anger can evolve into a state of well-being.

Suffering is virtually inevitable if we don't find a way to transform our anger from being harmful to beneficial. I attended a talk given by the peace activist and revered Buddhist teacher Thich Nhat Hanh, and I remember him saying that anger has the power to destroy or to strengthen us. He added that violent attitudes, including anger, even when expressed or acted out for understandable reasons, create more violence. As I looked into that statement, I could see its truth reflected in myself and in the outside world.

To paraphrase the words of Western Buddhist nun Pema Chödrön, when we act out, or get stuck in, our anger, we think we are getting back at the person who violated us.

However, when we look a bit closer, we'll see that holding onto that anger is like *eating rat poison and expecting the rat to die*—we're poisoning ourselves by carrying the toxicity that we believe we are giving to the one that violated us.

To deeply take care of ourselves, we need to become aware of the consequences of our habitual expression or suppression of anger and other resistant emotions. There is a strong pull in all of us to stay with the story of how we were wronged, to share it with our friends, and to justify our reaction. Many of us get absorbed, and allow these feelings to take over our thoughts, emotions and even our body's response. While our story may sometimes be an accurate reflection of what happened, the conflict that we continue to perpetuate through our resistant reactions does not serve our well-being or fulfillment.

Focusing Awareness on Our Anger

Most of us are only aware of the destructive side of our anger at the level of fleeting or intellectual awareness. This is because bringing awareness with a healing intention toward anger *while it's happening* is much more challenging.

Some of us who were brought up in a conflict-avoidant environment usually either reject ourselves with an internal dialogue that says something like, "I shouldn't feel this way," or we will have learned to suppress our conscious experience of it entirely.

If we can bring awareness that heals to our anger, we can begin to explore the reasons why it's triggered. As we learn how to do that, we realize that anger can be a tool for awakening to what we truly need. Instead of working *against* us, our anger can work *for* us. As we start to truly grasp, with a deeper level of awareness, that spontaneously expressing our anger, agitation, irritation, frustration or impatience almost inevitably creates harm, we can then ask, "What is a better alternative?" The rest of this chapter answers that question.

Reflection Point: Can you remember a time in your life when you were angry and didn't become aware of it until later?

Taking It Deeper: Can you identify some of the resistant emotions (impatience, irritation, intolerance, frustration, etc.) that occur most frequently with those you love? Is there a pattern of how you respond to them?

The decision to develop your capacity to find your healing intention involving your anger and other resistant emotions becomes a lot easier to make if you keep in mind the self-evident truth: we would virtually always prefer to feel good instead of bad. This becomes crystal clear when you reflect on how your anger has sabotaged and hurt your life throughout the years. The stakes are extremely high. If you really see this, you will want to develop the practice that will enable you to feel peace in a more sustaining way.

When you don't feel you have a choice because of the potency of the anger, you need to establish ongoing reminders that originate from wisdom guidance, such as:

- In the midst of negativity, if I just act it out I'm going to suffer further.
- I would much rather live a contemplative and sensible life than a blindly reactive one.
- Punishment will only produce more punishment.

It's challenging to break instinctual patterns of aggression, especially in times of anger, impatience, intolerance or when we feel threatened. As discussed in Practice Five, this is where tuning into our wisdom guidance can be invaluable.

Containment: Pivoting from Creating Harm and Moving Toward Healing

I am proposing a paradigm shift that involves neither *suppressing* these challenging feelings nor *expressing* them negatively or aggressively. Instead, we can learn how to feel our anger and other resistant emotions in a way that doesn't create harm to ourselves or others and find a healthy way to experience them. I call this process *containment*.

As they begin to work with containing their anger, many of my clients initially confuse containing it with suppressing it. They also frequently see that it takes them a while to adjust from their long-term patterns of dumping their anger outward to becoming aware of what made them mad in the first place. All of this is likely to be true for you, too. It's worthwhile, then, to ask yourself to be on the alert for your own views about expressing anger and for your patterns as you read about this alternative way of experiencing and expressing it.

All of us feel an almost instant relief when we express our anger in an immediate way: we develop a false sense of benefit—but this doesn't last very long. On the other hand, containment helps us to both identify and experience our feelings. Further, it allows us to explore what lies beneath them and contemplate how to best support ourselves and those we love. It gives us space to feel the feelings fully without acting them out with a knee-jerk reaction—while continuing to engage an intention to heal.

Some of us might justify sharing our anger as, "I needed to express my truth." However, as Buddha has said, "Truth is only truth when it is constructive."

▼

Reflection Point: Think of some key moments when your gut instincts to express anger and resistant emotions have felt justified, but have led to an escalation of the situation. Can you recall at least one time where, even though the anger felt cathartic in the moment, it led to further pain and destruction?

Taking It Deeper: Do you know anyone in your life that paused when they were angry before expressing themselves? If so, did it help them to communicate in a more sensitive way to create a better option?

Containment does not mean acting falsely sweet or soft. Genuine containment will most often result in being strong and sensitive at the same time, while being clear about what you need. That is: you can express your strength in a way that still has a quality of ease and sincerity in it. It helps restore, re-channel and dignify the vitality and energy of your anger and its intensity—but it doesn't repress the emotions.

Think of containment as developing a way of having a relationship to our anger just at the moment when our tendency to blame others is strongest. *This is a crucial and pivotal moment, because we are learning how to witness and contain our reactivity and reaction against someone in order to look for and find what we really want or need.*

Practicing Containment

With containment, we are encouraging ourselves to experience the rawness of our anger and resistant emotions in a safe environment. As we do this, we become even more conscious and sensitive in how we respond to our feelings. Containment encourages a heightened experiential awareness that can allow us to be free to take actions and change attitudes that improve our relationships rather than reinforce an enduring inner or outer power struggle or conflict.

In order to avoid reactive engagement, you may need to physically leave the situation that has triggered your emotion and go to a safe and separate space. Once there, you can guide yourself to feel as fully as possible the anger, hatred, impatience, rage, coldness or contraction without judgment or self-recrimination. You may need to get your feelings out by doing a variety of things: screaming what you are angry at, hitting pillows, stomping, shaking your body, exercising, yelling along with your favorite "aggressive" music, journaling, creating art, etc. Whatever you do, make sure you are not distracting yourself from the emotion. The aim is to allow yourself to fully feel the emotion for as long as it takes until you are in touch with all of its elements. This is actually an act of profound self-care and is energizing when you deeply embrace it. It is not a performance, but rather permission to feel and express yourself as if you were in the situation that you are angry at or impatient about, or with the person with whom you are feeling upset. The more you feel it with every fiber of your being, the greater your chance is to access greater sensitivity and insight about what you need. This allows you to experience the anger with significantly reduced chances of creating harm.

If you aren't able to take yourself out of the situation, you will at least need to take your attention inwards to acknowledge and feel the emotion without making it overtly obvious to another or expressing it. When someone sparks your anger, you might find yourself *inwardly* shouting something like, "I hate your stinking attitude. I hate the way you act superior. I hate it, I hate it!" While you are with the person in question, it's very difficult not to show your feelings. As a safeguard to avoid further conflict and if you think it is likely to be seen by the person who provoked your anger, you might choose to say something along the lines of, "I'd like to pick this conversation up later," or "I'm upset and need to process my feelings before talking about them." These kinds of comments won't create the release we might be used to, and will no doubt be incongruent with what we feel. Some of us may even feel we're being dishonest by not letting the other person have our "truth." It is important to consider, as we will in this chapter, how much more constructive it is likely to be when we take the time to communicate with a more neutral or kind heart. I believe what will become evident is that this can be found through containment and accessing our essential needs.

Reflection Point: What is your reaction to the idea of containing your resistant emotions?

Taking It Deeper: Next time you are in a conflict, before acting out, try to remind yourself to pause and ask the question, "How can I best respond to this situation and my resistant emotions?"

Uncovering the Vulnerability Beneath Resistant Emotions

As we use awareness that heals and containment to transform our anger, there is another key insight: we begin to recognize the vulnerable feelings that lie beneath the resistant ones, such as our anger. Knowing this allows us to aim for something with more healing potential. This is the beginning of a major shift of moving from being against someone or something, to being able to feel more harmless and in touch with the feelings of our unmet needs. As you become more skilled at containing your anger and resistant emotions, a new door opens—and you can naturally assist this happening by asking yourself, "What feelings of vulnerability lie beneath?" As you practice containment, this becomes more and more automatic and authentic.

When we are experiencing intense resistant emotions during conflict with another, there are almost always some layers of fear, hurt, loss or other similar feelings that sit closer to our heart. Along with containing how we are feeling, we want to develop the capacity to look beneath the defensive or self-protective reasons for our emotions, and then find the needs and vulnerabilities that will support our healing. As we feel these vulnerable emotions, they bring us to a less resistant place where we can more easily begin to access our needs instead of blaming others. This enables us to shift the focus from being against the other person to facing our own pain, loss or fear.

It is also important to realize, as we explored in Practice Seven, that underneath our anger we will sometimes find desires rather than needs. We might be angry that we are left on hold on the telephone longer than we think is reasonable or that we lost money gambling. We might also be impatient or annoyed with another because we are wrestling with unresolved pain related to issues like our finances, health or other losses and fears in different relationships. These internal feelings can lead us to getting angry with another because it is hard to tolerate the more raw suffering. If we look closely, we sometimes might find desires, and at other times we might find needs inside ourselves that are not being satisfied. The work done previously on this distinction in the last chapter can help us in our practice of containment as we continue to look for what is underneath our anger.

Once we have discerned that we are dealing with our essential needs—and not our desires—we're in a position to go for them and take steps to either fulfill them or use our friendly mind to patiently support us until we can.

In my work in relationship counseling, two different sets of needs, one from each partner, are often presented. The tendency on the part of each partner to defend against their needs with resistant emotions or anger in order to protect their vulnerability is commonplace. Here is a case study that illuminates both the dangers of expressing resistant emotions (instead of containing them) and the benefits of accessing essential needs.

Janine and William

Janine and William came into the office and were questioning whether it was time to end their twenty-year marriage. They wanted to see if they could deal with both communication issues and the seemingly glaring differences that existed between what each of them most enjoyed in life.

Janine started by saying (with annoyance and irritation tainting almost every word), "He is just so enamored with his work, his possessions, concerts and social events that there is no real time for us or for me."

William began this first session loaded with criticism and accusation. "All she wants to do is stay home, read and spend time alone. She's isolated and I don't think she can ever be really happy."

I asked William if he could see the negative tone in which he was talking about her. After initial resistance to what I was saying, he admitted that he was condescending and belittling.

They both seemed stunned that we weren't focusing on the content of their remarks, but instead on the energy or aggression beneath the words that were causing their estrangement.

I asked Janine if she could hear the tone of her negativity and she acknowledged it. "But," she added, "it is so frustrating to see him putting so much energy and attention into all his activities leaving little or no time to be together." I asked if she could hear the attacking way that she was approaching him. She had been just focusing on the words and not hearing her tone.

For a part of the next session I invited them to each just express and experience (and if anything exaggerate) the resistance, repulsion, and judgment toward each other without inhibition. Both of them had a great sense of humor, taking it seriously and at the same time starting to laugh at themselves as they saw the absurdity of believing that lashing out and blaming each other was going to do anything other than create irreparable harm.

"Does it make sense to both of you," I asked, "that no one likes being talked to in this way? Can you see that you are guaranteed to alienate each other if you continue?" They both had become aware of their antagonism (Awareness) and began to stop rationalizing that it was deserved. They clearly recognized that it was a part of what had led to the hopelessness that they were both feeling.

They could see they really wanted to find a way to express themselves in a more positive way (Healing Intention) and were receptive when I asked them to do the best they could to feel what they felt privately or with me, but not to dump it on each other. (Containment) They did love each other, and were highly motivated to begin the process.

I also asked them if they were aware of how they felt when they heard the other's negative attitude, resistance and fight. During a few sessions, William expressed that he felt wounded and rejected that Janine did not join him in his favorite activities. Janine said she felt rejected and neglected because of his lack of expressed desire or caring for quality time alone. (Vulnerable Feelings)

As they shared these vulnerable feelings, they looked tearfully at each other with new eyes. Over the next several weeks, a growing tenderness emerged between them. This softening made it so much easier to convey what they needed, which was primarily acceptance, understanding and appreciation from each other.

As time went on it became increasingly clear that they were able to express their more caring and sensitive qualities toward each other. She graced him by embracing more of the ways that he loved to enjoy, and he had a greater respect and appreciation for the self-sufficiency and quiet joy that she embodied. Instead of avoiding her, he realized again that he loved connecting with her. They both saw very clearly that anger had blocked the expression of what each of them needed, and when they were able to hear the needs, they reconnected with their original love and depth of respect. As is almost always the case, this kind of deep support and caring led to a sensual intimacy that emanated from the closeness in their hearts.

When both William and Janine were able to sense their own vulnerability, it made it much easier for them to access their needs.

From Resistant Emotions to Needs: Seven Steps

Now that we have explored the difference between containing and suppressing or expressing anger, we can turn directly to the core process that will catalyze the transformation of anger and other resistant emotions. As mentioned earlier, the practice of moving from our resistant and aggressive feelings to our essential needs has seven key steps. While they have a natural order, they can also occur in any sequence. So, consider this as a guide, but not a rigid one.

1. *Awareness of anger or other resistant emotions*
The first step is to become aware of your anger, pause for a few moments, and acknowledge it to yourself. In essence, your friendly mind is saying, "It's great that you're aware of your anger so now you have a chance to work with it." Take the time to appreciate your awareness and savor the experience of feeling alive and aware. Your awareness may come to you in many ways, including your tone, tension in your body or your reaction to

an unexpected response from another.

I have found that we so often don't recognize our own anger and the many forms it can take. Encourage yourself to experience and stay aware of these feelings as fully as possible, either right now or when they arise, without expressing or suppressing them.

2. *Intention to heal*

Then say to yourself something like, "I am now refocusing toward what will give me the best way to use this energy to serve my life—without hurting myself or anyone else unnecessarily." Your focus shifts, first away from what you are feeling against or resistant to, and then toward how you can best move toward healing. You recognize all of the harm that has been created by either reacting with anger or suppressing it, and you remind yourself that you want to find a way to best relate to your anger *in a way that it can serve you, rather than enslave you.* You say something like, "I really want to move toward what is needed, rather than fight against what I don't like."

3. *Containing and feeling your anger*

As you choose to contain these aggressive feelings, you see that you need to take time to create a "safe zone" internally or in a place where you can be harmless to all involved, including yourself. In this safe place, you are free to support yourself and to experience the fullness of your anger or other resistant emotions. You may need to get your feelings out by expressing and experiencing yourself in the ways described earlier. Give yourself as much time as you need.

As I highlighted earlier, there will be many times where you won't have the opportunity of going to a separate environment. Then you will have to do your best to experience your anger internally, and not reveal your inner state in an untimely, unhelpful way. If it isn't clear whether you can achieve this, then you can acknowledge that you are going through some feelings and would like to talk about it later.

4. *Experiencing the vulnerability underneath your resistant emotions*

We know that vulnerable feelings are almost always underneath these strong emotions. To support yourself to find these feelings, you might ask yourself, "What vulnerable feelings are beneath my anger?" Even if you're not in touch with these feelings or don't experience them right away, persevere, using your growing understanding and confidence that they exist underneath. Spend some time contemplating that your anger is a defensive way of blocking feelings that are fragile, usually harder to bear, and are closer to your heart. Your contemplation may also reveal that the anger has blocked something that hurt or scared you, whether you were in touch with it or not. You can, therefore, know that each time you give yourself permission to feel what you resist, you also gain access to a part of yourself that is interested in what frightened or hurt you.

5. *Identifying and being in touch with your needs*

Ask yourself, "What is that need that made me so mad and vulnerable in the first place?" "What didn't I get or what did I receive that I didn't want?" Let yourself dwell in this inquiry until what you really need reveals itself. Use the **Underlying Needs/Essential Qualities** chart as often as you can—it will help you become familiar with them.

6. *Expressing your needs with sensitivity when there's a chance of being heard*

Once you become clear about what you need, reflect on the best timing and tone of voice to potentially express it. Seek to attune yourself sensitively to all those who are involved.

This step becomes relevant if the other people involved are receptive.

If you decide to communicate your needs, be very careful not to let that original anger pollute the tone in which you express them. As you can imagine, this requires delicate monitoring of yourself. Keep in mind that you might need to make several sincere efforts.

7. *Finding acceptance and peace when communication isn't possible*

Sometimes you will notice that your efforts at communication are futile. In these cases, you will want to ask yourself, "How can I best deepen my acceptance—or at least tolerance—recognizing that I have already tried my best to communicate my needs without any positive outcome?"

There are several ways to accomplish this. Accept the impasse for now—and maybe forever. Recognize that it may not be a large issue in the broader context of a relationship that is still otherwise very worthwhile. This experience may also lead you into greater independence. Your newfound reality may be that you can't share an important area that you previously believed was possible.

Here is a list of the steps:

From Resistant Emotions to Needs: Seven Steps
1. Awareness of anger or other resistant emotions
2. Intention to heal
3. Containing and feeling your anger
4. Experiencing the vulnerability underneath your resistant emotions
5. Identifying and being in touch with your needs
6. Expressing your needs with sensitivity when there's a chance of being heard
7. Finding acceptance and peace when communication isn't possible

When you are able to work through these steps and practice the alchemy of transforming anger into healing and access to your needs, see if you can allow yourself to appreciate what you have just done. Can you see that moving your anger through these stages toward your underlying needs is a major breakthrough, and in some ways, like a miracle?

I mentioned earlier that this process is not linear or fixed: it is a fluid process that moves in its own rhythm and unfolds according to what best serves a specific situation and your temperament.

Healing Our Resistant Feelings

Working with our awareness and our deep-seated wish to heal often makes us aware that our resistant emotions require further attention. This section will look closely at these emotions and how we can find our vulnerability and underlying needs.

You'll see from the next examples and case study that following the seven-step process isn't an absolute guarantee for getting the outcome we seek. The external world does not always give us what we want even when we are skillful in our efforts. When this happens, our focus can be on finding ways to care for ourselves—and do our best to fulfill our needs internally when possible. I encourage you to focus closely on whichever of these examples of resistant emotions is most relevant to your own challenges and to look for where you might normally get caught in reactions that don't serve you.

Example #1:
John discovered that the broker running his investments was taking a large and undisclosed profit. Technically, he might have been legally entitled to it, but John felt outraged by the lack of

transparency and the fact that a decision had been made without his knowledge—and it was one that that he would never have agreed to. (Awareness)

John knew he wanted to focus on what qualities were needed so that he would have the best chance to be treated fairly. (Intention to Heal) He encouraged himself to take his time and feel both the anger long enough to discover what he needed, and what vulnerable feelings might lie underneath. (Containing Anger) He realized that he was deeply hurt and felt betrayed by the seeming dishonesty and greed on the part of the broker. (Experiencing Vulnerability) He inquired how he could best communicate or respond. (Identifying Needs)

When John called his broker, he didn't lash out with accusations—nor was he passive. With evenness in his tone he said, "I am confused about how you came to these numbers. Can you walk me through them?" (Expressing Needs with Sensitivity) As he saw the inaccuracies in what his broker presented, he asked with sincerity for clarification, as it seemed that the costs that were listed were more than customary. After patiently going through a few rounds of listening to the broker's rationalizations, he was able to negotiate a reduction in the extra fees. Instead of creating antagonism, John worked with his broker until the numbers were finally adjusted. He knew that if he had just reacted emotionally, it would have ended in a fruitless and antagonizing power struggle.

Example #2:
Alice was irritated because she sensed that her partner, Laura, had been withdrawn and she wanted to know what the cause was. (Awareness) As she considered what to do, she knew she didn't want to be bluntly accusatory or tense. She wanted to find a way

that would create intimacy. (Intention to Heal) After all, she wasn't even sure her feelings were right or even if Laura's change had anything to do with her.

Alice took some time alone for a couple of days to allow herself to feel everything she could to get in touch with her needs. (Containing Anger) She recognized that she was afraid of being hurt and rejected by what Laura might say. (Experiencing Vulnerability) She knew she needed to know the truth and contemplated how it could lead to more connection and intimacy with Laura. (Identifying Needs)

"I'm wondering if you have been withdrawing from me lately," Alice asked Laura at an appropriate moment. "Would you be open to telling me how you see it? And if you agree, would you let me know what's going on?" (Expressing Needs) Laura acknowledged that she'd been withdrawn and let Alice know what she needed. Alice listened and was relieved to find that what she wanted was more shared responsibility with their kids and housework. Alice saw these requests as reasonable. This led her to really relax. As she experienced this, Alice acknowledged that she had let Laura down and felt bad about how much she had withdrawn her affection. For Laura, Alice's acknowledgment of her withholding was a surprising gift. This allowed their relationship to deepen.

Reflection Point: Consider your openness to engaging a healing intention when you are angry. At this stage, being receptive to this idea is its own success. Notice how you experience the step of contemplating this.

Taking It Deeper: See if you can identify a conflict in one of your principal relationships where you might make a shift toward expressing sincerely what you need. What would you say? How would you say it?

Example #3:

Matthew had given his nephew a loan to finish a project on his house with a clear deadline. When the deadline passed with no payment or communication, Matthew felt angry that his patience, generosity and goodwill were being ignored. (Awareness)

He processed his angry feelings with a close friend to help him support the attitudes that would serve his needs. (Intention to Heal and Containing Anger) He discovered that he felt a deep sense of abandonment and wounding because he had been so taken advantage of. (Expressing Vulnerability) This helped him stay focused on firm and fair boundaries and sensitive communication when he and his nephew needed to sign papers to extend the loan. (Being in Touch with Needs) Matthew did *not* say, "I am really upset that you seem to be taking me for granted." Instead, he said, "I would really appreciate you directly talking with me. If you want to extend the loan, let's discuss fair terms." He paid careful attention to maintaining a neutral and even-tempered tone. (Expressing Needs with Sensitivity) He ended up writing a contract that, even though it was uncomfortable for him, meant that he and his nephew could come to an agreement. While he was clear that he wouldn't make a loan like this again, he had prevented a family rupture. He felt it was his best option, knowing that this allowed for the best outcome possible.

Jake

Jake came into my office complaining about an issue with his stepson, Tim. He experienced Tim as lazy and unmotivated. Basically, he felt he was not coming even close to fulfilling his potential. Jake was going back and forth between being irate and withdrawn. (Awareness) He believed the cause of his suffering was his anger about the "impossible" situation he was facing. Moving his focus from the outside situation to his inner reality, I asked him a question I have found extremely useful when working with someone who is feeling anger or withdrawal: "Do you like how you are approaching him, and do you think this is the wisest way to do it?" He responded, "No," and chuckled at the absurdity. "Of course I don't like being uptight and isolated. I don't think it's helpful, either. I know I need to find another way of responding. However, I am pissed off with Tim and I don't want to deal with the situation: I want him to change."

I encouraged Jake to explore his anger and frustration in relationship to his stepson and see if he could find the source. Gradually, during our sessions, he recognized that he was having a great deal of difficulty accepting what he grew to understand were Tim's limitations. As a highly motivated and successful person himself, Jake found it difficult to understand why his stepson couldn't make more of an effort to step up his game and get things done. I pointed out to him that he had provided his stepson with all the best opportunities such as psychiatrists, psychologists and teachers and yet they had all "failed" to make progress.

The stepson had been diagnosed with a major chemical

imbalance, and Jake's standards were completely unrealistic. Once he was able to find empathy and an acceptance of Tim's unchangeable developmental and neurological deficits, Jake was able to accept him so much more than he had been able to before. (Containing Anger) He still felt a deep helplessness, but it was a major upgrade from the anger he'd felt because he'd been so caught up in both his rejection of Tim, and his own self-rejection that he'd experienced once he realized what he was dealing with. (Experiencing Vulnerability) He found a sense of calm in letting go of trying to force impossible changes on his stepson—one of the main sources of his own frustration and anger. Even though his stepson didn't come close to fulfilling all his wishes for him, he found an empathy and respect for what Tim had to deal with and an acceptance that allowed for the best possible relationship between them. (Identifying Needs) Following this, as he felt Jake's kindness and support, Tim was able to achieve some significant success.

Just like Jake at the beginning of this case study, when we judge someone else's actions or attitudes, it almost never enters our minds that perhaps it is our *own* emotional reactions that need a closer examination. In carrying our judgments, we fail to recognize how they create suffering and burden.

Benefits and Teachings from Transforming Anger

And now, in this final case study (which demonstrates all the steps), we'll take a closer look at exactly how this seven-step process of transforming anger can enrich our lives. Here is how one couple applied the process to their marriage.

Adam and Celeste

Adam's typical complaint about his wife was that Celeste was "self-centered." He wished she would devote "more time to opening her heart and communicating and connecting. She is too busy with the kids and the rest of her life." With exasperation and intolerance in his voice, he would say to her, "You're really so self-involved, and I don't think you even care about what I ask for!"

"Are you aware of how angry you are toward Celeste as you speak?" I asked him.

From his replies, it became clear that he was not conscious of that at all. After going through a couple of rounds of him feeling "justified given the circumstances," he began his journey of becoming more aware of his resistant emotions.

I asked him if he could see whether or not he was using his tone or words in a way that would sabotage the very message he wanted to give. He knew he wanted to ask for more consideration; he saw instead that he was complaining and indicting her character. He got it. (Awareness) He said with slight self-deprecation, "I do want to go beyond my own bellyaching." (Intention to Heal)

Through time and persistent questions that focused on what else he felt, Adam became increasingly capable of sharing his feelings of abandonment, hurt, loneliness and his desire to be intimate. (Containing Anger and Experiencing Vulnerability) His transformation from expressing complaint to expressing vulnerability eventually allowed and encouraged Celeste to begin opening her own heart. As she no longer felt like she was being attacked, she could feel his pain rather than just his judgments. As a result, she was also able to express her own feelings of failure, underlying anxiety, and inadequacy that she had carried with her throughout her life. (Experiencing Vulnerability)

"What is it that you really need from her?" I asked Adam gently. It's a question I continued to ask.

It took several months, but he gradually became able to respond to my question as he gained an understanding of what his needs were, and could distinguish them from his emotions. (Identifying and Being in Touch with Needs) He found that it was helpful to review the **Underlying Needs/Essential Qualities** chart: he could see which of them applied to him. From there, he was able to ask Celeste to be present, soft and emotionally transparent with him. This was a huge shift—he went from being reactive to proactive in caring for his own well-being in a way that was harmless and clear to her. (Expressing Needs with Sensitivity)

Celeste also worked on how she came across in the relationship. Prior to the beginning of his exploration, Celeste had shared with me that she had found Adam to be needy. "He's so needy that it's really a turnoff. I wish he could be more whole

within himself without thinking I'm the source of his happiness."
(Awareness)

"Can you see how judgmental you are regarding Adam's
needs?" I asked her.

She was a bit confused when she acknowledged her
judgments, but as is usually the case she said, "Well, who wouldn't
be when he's so needy?"

It took some time for her to really see that not only were his
needs valid, but that she was sabotaging the communication with
her snide tone. She conveyed in several ways that she knew she
wanted to do better. (Intention to Heal and Containing Anger) In
one of those early sessions, I asked her, "What are the vulnerable
feelings present underneath your judgments of Adam—those that
perhaps have little to do with him directly?"

This was very difficult for her at first. She was bewildered
by my question. She began by acknowledging a feeling of
aversion to closeness which she recognized was a compensation
for the extreme loneliness she had been accustomed to in her
childhood. Celeste told me that she felt constantly anxious that
she might never have a heart big enough to care for her kids
and her husband at the same time. She expressed, "I feel really
inadequate and depleted at the end of every day." (Experiencing
Vulnerability)

When I asked her to reveal her feelings and let me feel her
anxiety and feelings of inadequacy as much as she could, she
began to feel nauseous. She felt like she was going to throw up
during the rest of the session. She told me, "I feel so anxious and
inferior about my inability to love." (Experiencing Vulnerability)

I asked Celeste to consider opening up in slow motion at home with Adam and sharing what was underneath the surface of her conscious experience throughout the day. Together, we found a way that led to her expressing her vulnerability and needs and asking him to just be with her without trying to "fix" her. (Expressing Needs)

Separately, I asked Adam to be receptive to a new level of her sharing of her vulnerability. By being able to see and experience her own vulnerability, Celeste could see that what she was judging as needy in Adam also applied to her. She saw that he was expressing his needs, and she was judgmental because she hadn't been aware of her own. (Awareness)

To help stabilize the insights that they gained, I stopped each of them numerous times when they were being negative toward each other. I asked that they reflect on how else they might be able to speak about their vulnerability and the expression of their needs from their hearts. At first, I needed to stop them on an ongoing basis and ask for contemplation. (Containing Anger) After a few months, they started to get the hang of it and they were mostly smiling, stopping themselves from feeling the negativity, and inquiring about their vulnerability and their needs. Celeste expressed numerous times her need to be accepted and cared for in her anxiety. Adam was able to ask her to share her vulnerability, rather than withdrawing or attacking. Both of them were living in a new aliveness based on asking for and receiving what they needed.

Following these breakthroughs and over the next few weeks, both of them shared with me that they were loving each other emotionally and sensually in ways that exceeded their honeymoon fifteen years earlier. Their journey forward continued because they had found ways to acknowledge their resistant emotions, find their vulnerability, share it along with their needs and requests, and do their best to stay open. Celeste and Adam were making leaps and bounds in learning to transform their anger and resistant emotions as part of their individual growth; the result was a vastly expanding intimacy in their relationship. This mixture of awareness of resistant emotions and vulnerability, followed by the honest expression of essential needs and compassionate sensitivity, are some of the most potent ingredients in genuine love.

As this case study shows, the practice of transforming anger—and all the resistant emotions that may be intertwined—is a powerful, potentially healing and intimate process. Some key lessons deserve to be highlighted:

- The first fundamental step is to honestly face your relationship to anger. Consider how your relationship to anger (and other resistant emotions) has caused harm for both yourself and others.
- Transforming anger is built on awareness that heals. Cultivating that awareness is a vital part of this (and every other) practice. You can then find your way to make the ultimate turnaround to have anger and resistant emotions serve your life by accessing your intention to heal, rather than having them create damage.
- Containment is the key pivot when moving from anger toward our underlying needs. Only by finding a way to contain your anger can you then discover your less volatile and more vulnerable feelings and needs. You can then move from fighting against what you

don't want to going for what you do want, which is meeting your true needs. Remember that you also need to engage your awareness, humility and honesty in the heat of the moment—when you most want to strike back—so you can create benefit rather than harm.

- By communicating what you need most in a sensitive way, rather than provoking endless conflicts or withdrawing in bitterness, you activate the potential for communication with those closest to you. When that is not possible, you can continue to work with your own anger internally—when it is the only way to take care of yourself.

Reflection Point: How often do you feel you are aware enough to bring an intention to heal while a resistant emotion is happening?

Taking It Deeper: Once you have accessed your intention to heal, how much do you believe you can communicate what you need in a sensitive way? Remember that in the beginning, the original anger is likely to sneak in. The more aware you are of this, the better chance you have that you will be able to hone in on your tone of voice.

Key Messages

Transforming anger and resistant emotions is indeed an evolutionary step that most of us have not yet made. As you can see, bringing this practice into our lives would have immeasurable healing effects on us as individuals—and on the world.

When we understand that anger is a signpost that can show us our vulnerability, it becomes an access point to find our needs for love, communication and peace. Understanding anger in this way requires practice and practice and more practice. It requires that we forgo our stories about how entitled we are to hold on to our anger. We need to learn that even when we are right in some aspect or another, we aspire to find peace. It is my greatest hope that, no matter where you find yourself in relation to your anger or resistant emotions, you'll be able to use the tools in this chapter—particularly containment.

Containment requires a great deal of experimentation before it becomes authentic and moves toward becoming your go-to response. It is difficult for most of us to embrace this at first because we are so conditioned, through early life modeling and life's experience, to either express or suppress our anger. I have witnessed that containment has been a major turning point for everyone who's practiced it. My clients' main feedback, even as they saw containment's power and benefits, has been that considerable practice is required, but it's really worth it.

Containment starts the shift toward being *for* something or someone rather than against. It is the source of optimism and hope on more fronts than we can imagine. We are not passive in any way; rather, containment allows for a constructive power and passion that unleashing or suppressing our anger can never have. When we can experience anger with awareness, we can appreciate the wonderful alive energy it holds. Then it can be transformed for the benefit of our lives—and the lives of those around us.

Containment allows us to move toward experiencing our essential qualities and best nature when we are angry. It increases our chances that we won't revert to suppression or simply dumping our feelings outward. Isn't this where we would rather be?

Transforming your anger, then, is a major piece of personal and interpersonal work that has the power to not only change your relationship to anger, but also your relationship with everyone that it arises with. And by extension, it creates hope and peace, not only in our singular worlds, but in the greater world we all live in.

Integrating the Chapter: Inquiries

1. How do you typically handle recurring anger-provoking situations in your life? What is the most important next step to support you in transforming your anger?
2. What are the vulnerable feelings that most often lie beneath your anger and resistant emotions? (For example, insecurity, hurt, rejection, abandonment or anxiety.)
3. What are the underlying, unmet needs that lead you most often to anger and resistant emotions?
4. When the significant others around you get upset with you, can you attune to their unmet needs?

For additional support and further integration of Practice Eight, I strongly encourage you to listen to the guided meditations at www.AwarenessThatHeals.org.

CONCLUSION

Making the Practices Your Own

*We want to keep being as present as possible
and focus on the next step toward healing
without any illusion of arriving.*

A s you began this book, you may have felt that you were reading a
book about *my* practices. But by the time you reach the final page,
my wish is that they will also be *yours*.

I hope that you feel uplifted by the many practices that can transform
challenges into opportunities. When it feels impossible to get there, I trust
that your friendly mind will be ever more available and helpful. This alone
will allow you to be more connected to yourself and the life you most
want, no matter what you are going through. As I have said throughout
this book multiple ways: *Who wouldn't be better off if they were able to listen to the most helpful, simplest and friendliest guidance—especially when
they are in the most challenging situations in life?*

Perhaps for you, it will feel most natural to take one or two of the
practices that particularly resonate and develop them more fully. Or
you may see this more as an interweaving of practices that you want to
integrate into your life as a whole. I offer you the following summary to

help illuminate the key elements of each practice and make them more accessible to you when you need their support.

Cultivating Awareness That Heals

Awareness of our challenges combined with an intention to heal and care for ourselves gives us the capacity to evolve toward our essential qualities. This evolutionary and rare combination changes our lives.

Using Friendly Mind Whenever Needed

Friendly mind can be our greatest inner resource when we are facing feelings or obstacles that we experience as impossible to overcome. We shift our attention toward what is possible and to how our thoughts can guide us to take care of ourselves. This process is more reliable than being led by challenging feelings that in turn will generate thoughts that will create more suffering.

Moving from Self-Rejection toward Self-Compassion

Self-rejection is far more common than we think. When we're caught in a challenging feeling or situation, asking skillful, heartfelt questions to see how much, if at all, we're actually caring for ourselves is a central way for finding out where our self-rejection may be hiding. This awareness, along with our intention to heal, sets us on the path toward developing self-acceptance, self-caring and self-compassion.

Inquiring from Our Hearts

Inquiry is frequently the best practice to enable us to refocus our attention when we're caught in difficult thoughts and emotions. Learning how to ask ourselves healing, supportive questions will open us to new options to move toward healing and fulfillment.

Listening to and following Our Wisdom Guidance

Accessing our awareness that heals and inquiring from the heart lead us to our most grounded wisdom. It will guide us with simple thoughts that have compassionate qualities and responses embedded in them.

Awakening to Our Tone of Voice

Becoming aware of how we sound when we speak and being attentive to the way others sound to us will illuminate a major source of suffering. With this awareness, we will naturally be drawn to our intention to heal that will guide us to using healing tones that will change the quality of our inner lives as well as our relationship to others.

Exploring Challenging Feelings to Find and Embrace our Essential Needs

When we understand the miraculous connection between our challenging feelings and essential needs, we are guided in the direction which allows us to best take care of ourselves.

Containing and Transforming Anger

When we are aware of our anger, accessing our intention to heal allows us to contain it. This opens the door to transforming the most potentially destructive energy inside us into vulnerability, healing and strength. We discover and go for what we need.

All of the practices in this book enable us to take care of ourselves in any given situation or with any given feeling. Rather than giving our primary attention to what we can't do, we naturally guide our attention toward what is actually possible.

Final Thoughts

Every challenge, every situation, every seemingly insurmountable roadblock is a key opportunity to use your awareness that heals. As you use these eight practices, you will gain an ongoing sense of being the *responder* to challenging situations and feelings instead of being consumed by them or reacting to them in ways that hurt you and others.

I speak to you with a vulnerability that is still a part of my life. It is now almost two decades since my kidney transplant. Through a combination of the practices in the book as well as solving some of the serious chemical issues going on in my body, I am experiencing a new kind of peace and inspiration during the majority of my days. The sheer beauty of knowing that I lost something so essential as my capacity to feel the richness of life, and that I found my way back to it, has given me a deeper gratitude and appreciation for life. And knowing, also, that I can lose it again, and that I have practices to use at those times, only adds to my sense of peace and encouragement.

However, life's challenges persist in significant ways. Every day I have a few challenging hours as I wake up in states of exhaustion and weakness. These are the times when I need and use friendly mind the most. It serves me by telling me, "I'm sorry that you have to feel this again and I know how unpleasant it is. You can trust in knowing that this is temporary, and the morning is the hardest part of every day. Even though it almost always feels permanent, you know it isn't. You also know that it's during the hardest times that you do your best work on yourself. I trust you ... and I am with you."

I feel a profound gratitude that my brother gave me his kidney. It gave me the opportunity to develop the capacity to live this life with the steady guidance of awareness that heals and the other practices that we have explored. I am so relieved and appreciative to be able to share my gratitude with my brother, and to share other elements of love and compassion with a wide range of people close to me.

For me there is no ultimate, final mastery of these practices. We want to keep being as present as possible and focus on the next step toward healing without any illusion of arriving. When we're thinking we have to arrive, we're setting ourselves up to fail. None of us, I believe, will ever arrive at a place where we can reliably and flawlessly care for ourselves at every one of our most difficult life passages. Appreciating this reality can support an inspired humility that keeps us alert to greet life as it is and be ready to care for ourselves when the next challenging surprise appears.

It might appear that it is self-centered to be oriented toward so much "self-compassion." But how we treat ourselves on the inside is going to be a major influence in how we treat the outside world. It is utterly paradoxical that the more we find this kind of inner trust and kindness, the more benefit we will naturally express in and for the world.

This book does not, as I mentioned earlier, present a *quick fix*. Instead, it presents a *realistic path with practices that support awareness that heals no matter what the conditions are*. Up to and including the day we die, we will face challenges that test us. Knowing that we can access the best of our inner guidance and resources when those times come will lead us to living in confidence, resiliency and strength. This is my heartfelt wish for all of us.

Glossary

AWARENESS

Its Four Levels

1. Being aware that we aren't aware of certain life challenges helps us to be curious and receptive.
2. Fleeting Awareness includes insights that we have that are short lived, spontaneous epiphanies.
3. Intellectual Awareness involves being aware of what is happening emotionally to others and ourselves in a stable way, but we have no clear motivation towards healing.
4. Healing Awareness involves being not only aware of our present challenging feelings, but also of a genuine motivation to move towards healing.

AWARENESS THAT HEALS

Awareness that heals is the experience of simultaneously being aware of what is challenging us in the present and accessing a healing intention that looks for what is realistically possible.

CHALLENGING FEELINGS AND EMOTIONS

These are equivalent in meaning. They have a sense of incompleteness or suffering to them, i.e., fear, loneliness, grief or anger. These are different from healing qualities and needs.

FEELINGS TO NEEDS

We are able to identify our challenging emotions and feelings and use them to reveal the specific, underlying needs that will be most healing and supportive in whatever difficult situation we are facing. (See Introspective Guides: Charts One, Two, and Three.)

FRIENDLY MIND

This is one of our greatest inner resources, especially at times when we are facing significant challenges or difficult emotions and can't feel peace or a sense of well-being. Our friendly mind guides us with responsive thoughts that allow us to best support ourselves with a next realistic step, movement or thought. At any time that we are suffering, even in the most extreme ways, these guiding thoughts will always be realistic and supportive, even if they don't necessarily feel friendly or compassionate. Friendly mind will bring us enormous relief because we aren't asking ourselves to do the impossible—which is to change how we feel. We are simply and sensibly guided by our best thoughts and not our challenging feelings.

HEALING INTENTION

It is our utmost sincere wish or longing to bring heart, mind and body to receive healing that can be most beneficial when we are meeting life's challenges.

NEEDS, QUALITIES OR ESSENTIAL NEEDS AND QUALITIES

These are identical in meaning. They represent the most essential elements of fulfillment and compassion, i.e., love, trust, strength.

NEEDS VERSUS DESIRES

Needs are essential to our fulfillment, and desires are either discretionary pleasures or harmless enjoyments.

RESISTANT FEELINGS/EMOTIONS

These emotions have resistance and fight in them, i.e., anger, impatience, irritation, passive aggressiveness and punishing withdrawal. See Introspective Guides: Chart Three, **Challenging Feelings and Emotions**, for additional examples.

VULNERABLE FEELINGS/EMOTIONS

These are our softer emotions that don't have resistance in them such as sadness, fear or loss—they focus on our inner experience and do not include blaming or being negative toward anyone. See Introspective Guides: Chart Three, **Challenging Feelings and Emotions**, for more examples.

WISDOM GUIDANCE

Wisdom Guidance comprises specific thoughts which embody the healing qualities; they encourage us in whatever situation we are facing.

Three Introspective Guides

You can download these guides
or purchase them, laminated, on
www.AwarenessThatHeals.org.

Introspective Guide - Chart One

UNDERLYING NEEDS/ESSENTIAL QUALITIES

As we use them here, needs and essential qualities are identical: they are all elements of compassion. This list can help you identify them so you can use them in more exacting and healing ways in your life.

abundance	friendliness	peace
acceptance	fulfillment	positivity
affection	generosity	presence
appreciation	gentleness	receptivity
attention	gratitude	recognition
authenticity	growth	reflection
awareness	happiness	relaxation
belonging	harmlessness	relief
calmness	healing	respect
communication	health	responsibility
compassion	helpfulness	safety
competence	honesty	satisfaction
confidence	hope	security
connection	humility	sensitivity
containment	humor	sexuality
contemplation	independence	silence
contentment	innocence	soothing
cooperation	inspiration	strength
courage	integrity	success
creativity	intimacy	support
discipline	kindness	tenderness
ease	love	tolerance
empathy	meaning	trust
encouragement	mutuality	understanding
esteem	openness	well-being
faith	patience	witnessing

Introspective Guide - Chart Two (1 of 4)

FROM CHALLENGING FEELINGS TO ESSENTIAL QUALITIES/NEEDS

HOW TO USE THIS CHART

- All the sequences on the right begin with becoming aware of your challenging emotion and accessing a Healing Intention. Please assume this ongoing and know they are not included in order to simplify the chart.
- Identify your specific challenging emotion in the left-hand column.
- Consider how the corresponding needs/qualities on the right relate to you specifically in your life regarding the particular feeling you have identified.
- Give yourself permission to change the order or the name of any specific quality so it feels right. The chart is not a directive but a guide, so you're likely to find some of the sequences or qualities you are contemplating don't apply, and you may also see something to add that works better for you.
- Recognize that both short- and long-term challenges are covered, but for almost all of us, long-term, chronic challenges will have a more gradual development of the qualities that will most help. Short-term situations will usually involve less time and not require the same amount of gradual engagement with as many healing qualities. But there are exceptions to both, and your use of the chart should be guided by a trust in your intuition to know what is best for you.

Challenging Emotion	Sequences of Underlying Essential Needs/Qualities
Abandonment	tolerance, acceptance, growth, tenderness
Aggression	containment, accountability, communication, calmness
Agitation	containment, tolerance, communication, peace
Alienation	containment, contemplation, communication, connection
Anger	containment, vulnerability, communication, strength

Introspective Guide - Chart Two (2 of 4)

Challenging Emotion	Sequences of Underlying Essential Needs/Qualities
Anxiety	tolerance, acceptance, tenderness, independence
Aversion	containment, tolerance, support, independence, cooperation
Bitterness	containment, tolerance, acceptance, inclusiveness
Coldness	containment, tolerance, ease, kindness
Condescension	containment, harmlessness, tolerance, mutuality
Competitiveness	containment, reflection, engagement, cooperation
Confusion	tolerance, reflection, discrimination, clarity
Contraction	containment, relaxation, understanding, peace
Dependency	reflection, growth, courage, independence
Depletion	tolerance, acceptance, tenderness, discrimination
Depression	tolerance, acceptance, discrimination, will
Despair	tolerance, acceptance, discernment, will
Disillusionment	tolerance, contemplation, discrimination, strength
Disappointment	tolerance, discrimination, acceptance, discipline, trust
Discouragement	tolerance, discrimination, will, acceptance, peace
Distrust	containment, contemplation, discrimination, trust
Domination	containment, honesty, harmlessness, cooperation
Embarrassment	acceptance, understanding, accountability, confidence
Emptiness	tolerance, acceptance, tenderness, growth, fulfillment
Exasperation	containment, discrimination, patience, well-being
Fear	tolerance, discrimination, safety, courage

Introspective Guide - Chart Two (3 of 4)

Challenging Emotion	Sequences of Underlying Essential Needs/Qualities
Frustration	containment, tolerance, acceptance, contemplation, peace
Grief	tolerance, acceptance, empathy, tenderness
Guilt	tolerance, discrimination, accountability, innocence
Helplessness	acceptance, contemplation, understanding, discipline, peace
Hopelessness	contemplation, tolerance, discrimination, will, acceptance
Hostility	containment, tolerance, acceptance, peace
Hurt	acceptance, tolerance, kindness, communication
Impatience	containment, tolerance, harmlessness, patience
Inadequacy	tolerance, acceptance, discrimination, warmth, growth
Inferiority	tolerance, acceptance, growth, peace, trust
Insecurity	tolerance, contemplation, growth, trust
Intolerance	containment, contemplation, accountability, humility, tolerance
Irritation	containment, acceptance, discrimination, relaxation, peace
Jealousy	tolerance, vulnerability, growth, self-compassion, trust
Judgment	containment, tolerance, discrimination, sensitivity
Loneliness	tolerance, growth, courage, connection
Loss	acceptance, silence, communication, tenderness
Moralism	discrimination, humility, sensitivity, compassion
Neediness	acceptance, growth, communication, independence
Pain	tolerance, acceptance, kindness, warmth
Pessimism	containment, discrimination, growth, trust

Introspective Guide - Chart Two (4 of 4)

Challenging Emotion	Sequences of Underlying Essential Needs/Qualities
Powerlessness	tolerance, discrimination, will, strength
Rage	containment, tolerance, harmlessness, strength
Regret	tolerance, contemplation, acceptance, growth, peace
Rejection	tolerance, kindness, growth, love
Remorse	acceptance, accountability, communication, trust
Repulsion	containment, tolerance, accountability, sensitivity
Resentment	containment, tolerance, honesty, equanimity
Sadness	acceptance, empathy, kindness, tenderness
Sarcasm	containment, acceptance, humility, growth
Self-hatred	containment, tolerance, encouragement, self-compassion
Selfishness	tolerance, contemplation, growth, generosity
Shame	tolerance, acceptance, accountability, self-compassion
Sickness	tolerance, comfort, tenderness, healing
Skepticism	reflection, curiosity, discrimination, trust
Sorrow	acceptance, warmth, gentleness, self-compassion
Superiority	containment, acceptance, growth, humility
Tension	tolerance, honesty, relaxation, trust
Wariness	discrimination, honesty, equanimity, trust
Weakness	tolerance, acceptance, growth, strength
Woundedness	tolerance, kindness, growth, self-compassion

Introspective Guide - Chart Three

CHALLENGING FEELINGS AND EMOTIONS

- Challenging feelings include both resistant and vulnerable emotions.
- Vulnerable feelings are softer and nonaggressive.
- Resistant emotions have fight and resistance in them.

Use the lists below to help you identify challenging feelings.
The descriptions are not intended to be all-inclusive or rigid in any way.

Resistant Emotions		Vulnerable Emotions	
agitated	impatient	abandonment	inferior
aggressive	intolerant	anxiety	incomplete
alienated	irritation	confusion	inhibition
angry	judgmental	dependency	insecurity
annoyed	moralistic	depletion	jealousy
antagonistic	pessimistic	depression	loneliness
aversion	power	despair	loss
bitter	rage	disappointment	needy
coldness	repulsion	discouragement	pain
competitive	resentment	disillusionment	powerless
condescension	resistance	embarrassment	regret
contracted	sarcasm	emptiness	rejection
disgust	self-hatred	fear	remorse
distrust	selfishness	grief	sadness
dominated	skepticism	guilt	shame
exasperation	superiority	helplessness	sick
frustration	tension	hopelessness	sorrow
hatred	violence	hurt	wanting
hostility	wariness	inadequate	weak

About the Author

*A*wareness *That Heals* is an expression of the tools that Robert Strock has developed over a lifetime of inspired self-exploration. During an almost five-decade practice as a teacher, psychotherapist, and humanitarian, he has developed a unique approach to communication, contemplation, and inquiry. Robert is the founder and chairperson of the Center for Authentic Living, which has distinguished itself as a leading counseling practice for the Southern California business, healing and entertainment communities. His many online videos are shared with therapists, psychology students, social workers, caregivers, and seekers of their own inspiration.

Twenty years ago, Robert co-founded the Global Bridge Foundation, whose mission is to work toward a more compassionate, peaceful world by offering guidance and funding that especially address poverty and global warming. This foundation aspires to be a part of a united effort—with other foundations—to support systems for global change and healing. Robert has taken his continuing lifelong self-exploration beyond his personal lifestyle and into inspirational work, both in his practice and the world.

Robert also created Psycho-Economics, which is a theory and practice designed to integrate our personal financial objectives with our life purpose in order to better align with our highest and truest values. By seeing more clearly where and how our money is used, and how it can align with our core priorities, we can see more clearly how fear can influence our financial goals and how to live a balanced work life.

Awareness That Heals brings to fruition the full expression of Robert's approach and the way he interacts with the many organizations and people in his daily work. He briefly summarizes it this way: "At all levels, I support my clients to cultivate a deepening kindness toward their emotional and practical challenges while simultaneously accessing their own best self whenever they are facing these issues. If I'm correctly doing my work, their best self is constantly interacting with their own pains and challenges.

"Given the state of our world, I have felt moved to take how I work with individuals and extend it to working with organizations and foundations: the issues are fundamentally the same."

Endorsements

In *Awareness That Heals* and The Guided Meditations, Robert weaves his experience in Spirituality and Psychotherapy to create an integrated tapestry of healing for spirit and mind. Buckminster Fuller said, "I seem to be a verb," and Robert gives readers and listeners the instructions for how to "verb" with integrity and in the right relationship to the larger whole. Robert has poured decades of experience and timeless love into this work that will enable you to boldly face the present moment. As we face a future of Utopia or Oblivion, it is vital that we heal our connections with ourselves, each other and the living planet we are part of. This book, meditations, and visualizations are a critical tool for the critical path toward a future that works for 100 percent of humanity.

—AMANDA JOY RAVENHILL, EXECUTIVE DIRECTOR, BUCKMINSTER FULLER INSTITUTE

At this moment in our nation's political history, we could all use a little healing. While we face existential threats on all sides, we must be mindful of how we're impacted, and of how we might work through that to achieve a better world for ourselves and our community. *Awareness That Heals* provides a practical road map for individual and collective healing so that we may show up to our communities restored and with intention.

—EZRA LEVIN, CO-EXECUTIVE DIRECTOR OF INDIVISIBLE

One of the unique gifts of *Awareness That Heals* is the remarkable range of its relevance. The benefits of reading this book are so deep and enduring because the practices enrich every level of our lives—personal, professional, even political.

—MARK GERZON, PRESIDENT, MEDIATORS FOUNDATION, CO-DESIGNER AND FACILITATOR OF THE US HOUSE OF REPRESENTATIVES BIPARTISAN CONGRESSIONAL RETREATS, AND AUTHOR OF *THE REUNITED STATES OF AMERICA: HOW WE CAN BRIDGE THE PARTISAN DIVIDE*

Awareness That Heals and The Guided Meditations capture Robert's heart, which I experienced whenever we met throughout the years, and I'm truly overjoyed that he's going public. I look forward to seeing the impact that this brilliant work will have in the field of psychology and most importantly, its broader implications for our troubled world.

—BARBRA STREISAND, ACTRESS, SINGER, DIRECTOR, PRODUCER, AND PHILANTHROPIST

When you are fortunate enough to work with Robert Strock, he passes his wisdom and loving awareness along so humbly that you discover that in truth, you are healing yourself. Further, when you stumble back into some darker crevices, you go to the gifts within his website—filled with rich resources—and you navigate even more as your own therapist, with Robert as your guide. Life is a lifelong process and my gratitude is reawakened constantly, as I am, within this work.

—SHERRY BROURMAN, PHYSICAL THERAPIST AND AUTHOR OF *WALK YOURSELF WELL*

If you ever feel alone, discouraged, and doubt your ability to change your own experience—much less the world at large—then this book is for you. What if you can reclaim your own peace, heal yourself and grow your compassion to help the world at large? That (and more) is what Robert Strock offers in his groundbreaking book and meditations, *Awareness That Heals*. I've personally had the benefit of working with this therapist and thought-leader when my own world felt dark. Now everyone can access Robert's deep caring and open heart through these easy-to-incorporate healings. You may never sit across from him in a therapy session, but when you hear his words read through his own voice, you'll feel as if you have.

—LEEZA GIBBONS, EMMY-WINNING TV HOST, BEST-SELLING AUTHOR, AND HEALTH ADVOCATE

True healing in a very real sense begins with merciful awareness. Robert Strock's very personal book reminds us that this boundless quality of our being can include every aspect of our self. No part left out.
—FRANK OSTASESKI, AUTHOR OF *THE FIVE INVITATIONS: DISCOVERING WHAT DEATH CAN TEACH US ABOUT LIVING FULLY*

Robert's decades of practice as both a devoted psychotherapist and dedicated Buddhist meditator uniquely qualify him to show in clear, plain language how to gently hold our suffering while simultaneously awakening our natural capacity for healing. By bringing universal spiritual values forward into the mainstream of best mental health practices, Robert has created new tools for caring—facets of the diamond of compassion to shine far and wide, illuminating our life and healing our world.
—TRUDY GOODMAN, PhD., AND FOUNDING TEACHER OF INSIGHT LA

As each of us confronts life's challenges, we can feel lost, or alone. Robert Strock's work provides unique healing strategies that bridge meditation, self-awareness, and develop our capacity to connect to ourselves, and the world. Robert speaks honestly about the exhaustion and anguish created by the severe chemical side effects of his kidney transplant and how the prior psychological tools he developed were insufficient. This inspired the new practices you will read, hear and see. *Awareness That Heals* is a powerful, vulnerable and honest companion to anyone coping with challenges big and small.

—SASHA DICHTER, CO-FOUNDER OF 60 DECIBELS, FORMER CHIEF INNOVATION OFFICER OF ACUMEN, BLOGGER ON GENEROSITY, PHILANTHROPY AND SOCIAL CHANGE, AND AUTHOR OF THE *MANIFESTO FOR NON-PROFIT CEOS*

Written and read aloud by one of the leading therapists and thinkers of our time, *Awareness That Heals* is one of the best guidebooks to achieving self-compassion and inner and outer peace ever written.

—KEN DRUCK, PH.D., AUTHOR OF *THE REAL RULES OF LIFE*, *COURAGEOUS AGING*, AND *HEALING YOUR LIFE AFTER THE LOSS OF A LOVED ONE*

Awareness That Heals draws on Robert's 45 years of experience as a psychotherapist to help people take a revolutionary approach to the areas of our greatest suffering. Robert is not afraid to openly share from his own "dark night of the soul" in order to help others. This book has helped me respond to the deepest stresses in my life by helping me find my instinct to care for myself, and at the same time, giving me several ways to move toward healing.

—Brent Kessel, CEO of Abacus Wealth Partners and Author of *It's Not About the Money*

In this multi-sensory experience (book, audio and audio-visual presentations), Robert Strock brilliantly and compassionately navigates the fathomless waters of psychology, spirituality, healing, mindfulness practice and the self-help movement without running aground or anchoring in a safe harbor any longer than necessary. *Awareness That Heals* is an invitation to a practical methodology that is both intellectually rigorous and emotionally satisfying. The combination of Awareness, Intention to Heal and Friendly Mind (as so beautifully presented in this collection) will become a guiding principle for me as my personal and professional life unfolds.

—Jack Lampl, Organizational Consultant, Mediator, Past President of Threshold Foundation, Past President of A. K. Rice Institute